IN
ONE
POT

Cook's notes

I like to use flaked sea salt, freshly ground black pepper and fresh herbs (unless otherwise stated). Eggs are medium-sized unless otherwise stated. The elderly, young children and anyone who is pregnant should avoid recipes that include raw or lightly cooked eggs. Timings in this book are for conventional ovens. If you are cooking with a fan-assisted oven, follow the temperature guidelines in this book but decrease the cooking time slightly.

First published in Great Britain in 2013
by Weidenfeld & Nicolson

10 9 8 7 6 5 4 3 2 1

Text © Blanche Vaughan 2013
Design and layout © Weidenfeld & Nicolson
Design & Art Direction by Julyan Bayes
Photography © Simon Wheeler
Illustrations by obroberts
Food styling by Claire Ptak
Proofread by Constance Novis
Index by Rosemary Dear

A CIP catalogue record for this book is available from the British Library.

ISBN: 978 0297 86745 6

Printed and bound in China
by C & C Joint Printing Co. Ltd

Weidenfeld & Nicolson
The Orion Publishing Group Ltd
Orion House
5 Upper St Martin's Lane
London WC2H 9EA

An Hachette UK Company

www.orionbooks.co.uk

The Orion Publishing Group's policy is to use papers that are natural, renewable and recyclable products and made from wood grown in sustainable forests. The logging and manufacturing processes are expected to conform to the environmental regulations of the country of origin.

WEIDENFELD & NICOLSON

IN ONE POT

Fresh recipes for every occasion

Blanche Vaughan

Photography by Simon Wheeler

CONTENTS

INTRODUCTION 6

QUICK POTS 17

Simple weekday suppers that don't take long

SLOW POTS 53

Comforting weekend dishes that you can spend more time on

LITTLE POTS 93

Good things to make for one or two

POTS TO GO 121

Portable food perfect for picnics or simple light lunches

PARTY POTS 149

Dishes to celebrate with

SWEET POTS 185

Puddings, cakes and delicious desserts

BASICS 223

A few things that will always come in handy

INDEX 236

ACKNOWLEDGEMENTS 240

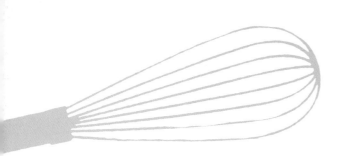

INTRODUCTION

This is real food, cooked simply and best of all — in one pot.

I love to cook for my friends and family, whatever the occasion — casual, quick suppers, healthy lunches or celebratory feasts with indulgent puddings. This book is about how to enjoy cooking by keeping things simple, preparing and serving everything in one pot, whether you're fitting time to cook into your busy life, or you just want to eat well.

What these recipes share is that they only require one main pot to be cooked or assembled in, be it a casserole, saucepan, roasting dish or frying pan. Aside from a good salad or bread to serve alongside, each recipe provides a meal in itself, all in one pot.

The roots of cooking began in one pot. Cooking in this way can be so full of possibility and variety and in its simplicity it can span many different cultures. There are curries from India, rustic home cooking from Italy and France, food you would find in the bustling markets of Turkey and Lebanon, as well as timeless British recipes. One-pot cooking can be quick and fresh — a simple salad made with vegetables and pearl barley, or something that is left alone to cook for hours, like a pot-au-feu of beef or gently braised lamb shanks. 'One pot' doesn't need to be limited to cooking in a huge cauldron. Some recipes like spaghetti al limone, meatballs in spiced tomato sauce or the Turkish-style eggs are for small amounts when you're cooking for just one or two. There are pots you can take with you on a picnic or into the office, like Japanese soba noodle salad with cucumber and sesame. There are recipes made for celebrations and for entertaining, like a chicken dish traditionally served in Morocco at New Year or a whole fish roasted on top of fennel and potatoes that you can simply put in the middle of

the table for everyone to help themselves. And finally, there are sweet pots — date and orange cake, little chocolate pots, tiramisu or baked or steamed fruit puddings — to delight all.

My hope is that these recipes will show new or less experienced cooks how simple the pleasures of food can be, as well as inspiring comfortable cooks to try some new recipes. Simple food can be the best to eat and the most enjoyable to cook. After all, being relaxed and having fun when you cook makes things taste better. These are recipes for people who like to eat well, who need some convenience in their lives and who can enjoy the informality of bringing a pot to the table to share among friends.

Blanche

KITCHEN KIT

As the title of this book suggests, cooking in one pot means not using too much equipment – and much less washing up! When it comes to pots and pans, I've always believed in quality over quantity. A really good pot is versatile and certainly worth the investment: get the basics right and you can do anything.

I'm not suggesting that you go out and buy everything on this list before you start cooking, because much of the fun is buying special pieces as you go along. However, these are just some ideas for handy kitchenware pieces that could be collected over time.

A medium-sized, heavy-based pot with a lid

Whether round or oval in shape, this will be the most useful item in your kitchen, so if you're going to splash out on one piece of kit, this is it. It's the one you will turn to time and time again to make everything from soups, risottos and pastas to fish stews and slow-braised meat. The unique thing about a heavy-based pot is that your ingredients cook more evenly, are less likely to burn and will produce a better all-round flavour.

Go for an ovenproof pot, made from enamel, cast iron or thick stainless steel. Look for solid handles and a sturdy lid. The size depends on the numbers you usually cook for, so use your better judgement. I have two very old Le Creusets (but other brands are just as good): a fairly large one in which I can pot roast a whole joint of pork and a smaller shallow one that I use to make risotto if there are only two of us. Nothing in my kitchen gets used more often.

Stockpot

You know what I mean: a really large deep pot that can accommodate a whole chicken for making stock, with room left for some vegetables around the sides, or a pile of mussels, which take up double the space when they are steamed open. Look for a stockpot with a good, solid base. It will conduct heat more evenly, meaning ingredients are less likely to burn. But if you're just going to fill it with liquid, for blanching vegetables, making stock or boiling salt beef or pot-au-feu, it doesn't have to be your most expensive piece of kit.

Heavy-based, shallow casserole

A cooking vessel with a wide base and low sides offers maximum heat contact. This shape is great for making anything where the liquid needs to be concentrated and reduced – like thickening a tomato sauce or letting a paella cook undisturbed while it soaks in the stock. I like one with a lid, like a tagine, so I can cook things covered, keeping the steam inside. Without the lid, a shallow casserole can become a pie dish, and you can arrange the pastry over the top in a layer.

Frying pan

It's good to have one small and one large frying pan. They are essential for everything from frittatas and pancakes to pork chops. Non-stick is not essential, just as long as the pan has a heavy base and, preferably, an ovenproof handle. This means you can use it for making tarte tatin or anything that starts on the stovetop and finishes in the oven.

Large roasting tray

An oversized rectangular tray (or roaster) with sides that takes up the whole shelf space of the oven is invaluable when you're cooking for a large group of friends or family. You can fit a whole fish in it, or a joint of meat surrounded by vegetables. A big tray will give your roast potatoes or vegetables lots of room to crisp up while they cook.

Oven dish

This includes any ceramic, glass or enamel oven dish that can be used both for cooking and for serving. It can be a perfect vessel for tiramisu, baked pears or clafoutis, for example. Plain and white or pretty and decorated, it will be a versatile piece of kit.

Little pots, tea cups or ramekins

These are the least essential and easiest to improvise, but it might be worth having one or two little ovenproof pots if you're partial to a baked egg or individual chocolate pot.

Pestle and mortar

I never use electric spice grinders, just a good old heavy pestle and mortar. They don't cost very much and last for ever. They are all you need for grinding spices or crushing garlic. If I've crushed garlic in it, I often whisk up my vinaigrette in the mortar too, rather than using a separate bowl to reduce washing up.

Stick blender

If you don't have a food processor and you like your soup velvety smooth, get a stick blender. Stick blenders are great for whizzing up an array of sauces or making mayonnaise and dressings. They're also easy to wash, much cheaper and more convenient in size than a standard food processor.

STORE CUPBOARD AND FRESH

Making great-tasting food at home relies on keeping your cupboards and fridge cleverly stocked. There are only a few staple ingredients every cook needs to have to hand, which make all the difference for achieving fuss-free meals. Here are some suggestions for what you might need in your store cupboard, and some essential fresh ingredients to make everyday cooking more convenient.

Olive oil

It's always good to have two types of olive oil: a lighter one for frying and cooking, and a really delicious (more indulgent) one for serving or making dressings with.

For cooking, you don't have to use olive oil – rapeseed or groundnut are other options. I prefer a light olive oil but let your taste guide you.

It's really worth buying a bottle of good-quality extra virgin olive oil for finishing a dish and to use in dressings. Whether it's delicately flavoured French or grassy Tuscan is up to you. I savour a really good olive oil in the same way that I appreciate a really good wine.

Rice and grains

No store cupboard is complete without rice and grains: they're healthy, filling and have a long shelf life. You don't always have to stick to the rice or grain suggested in the recipes that follow. If you don't like white rice, try brown, or use lentils instead of pearl barley. Explore your options. Afterall, experimenting is all part of the fun.

Salt and pepper

Sea salt flakes and freshly ground black pepper are the best things for seasoning. A trick I've learned is that if you season things at the beginning of cooking where it will really get absorbed, you'll use less salt. Fine sea salt is useful for salting water for pasta or blanching vegetables. It's less expensive and dissolves well.

Spices

A little spice goes a long way and can elevate a dish from plain to spectacular. Here's a guide to some essential spices that crop up a lot in this book. Buy in small amounts and use them while they're fresh.

* allspice berries
* cardamom
* chilli flakes
* cinnamon – stick and ground

* coriander seeds
* cumin – seeds or ground
* fennel seed
* fenugreek

* juniper berries
* mustard seeds
* nutmeg
* nigella seeds
* paprika powder

Tins, jars

Tinned or bottled vegetables, beans or pulses are excellent time-savers. I always try to keep my cupboards well stocked with:

* tomatoes – chopped or peeled plum
* beans – borlotti, cannellini and

butter beans
* anchovies – salted preferably, otherwise in oil

* chickpeas
* salted capers – but remember to rinse them before use

Vinegars

Good-quality vinegar can add a great deal to a dish. If I had to choose just two to have on my shelf, they would be sherry vinegar for its strength and red wine vinegar for its delicate acidity.

Dijon mustard

Great in both dressings and 'on the table' as a condiment, Dijon mustard is less intense than English mustard.

Tahini

A smooth, thick paste made from ground sesame seeds, with a rich, nutty flavour. Tahini is used a lot in Middle Eastern cooking and tastes especially good mixed with lemon juice and some olive oil to make a sauce for fish or meat.

A FEW FRESH THINGS ...

Garlic

Try to store garlic somewhere cool and dark (but not in the fridge) to prevent it from sprouting. If there is a green stem sprouting out or within the centre of the clove, remove it before cooking. Otherwise it could impart a harsh, rancid flavour into your dish.

Onions

I always have a good supply of onions, including a couple of red and couple of white ones. I find that if stored out of the fridge and somewhere cool and dark, they will also keep for longer.

Lemons

A squeeze of lemon at the end of cooking can do wonders to lift the flavours of a dish. A sprinkle of grated lemon zest will enliven just about any salad.

Ginger

Ginger, fresh or dried, is one of the greatest fresh spicy tastes and is used in many curries and dishes from the Far East. Slices of fresh ginger in hot water make a delicious and immune-boosting tea, too.

Red chilli

Chilli doesn't have to make dishes too hot. It's often useful to add just a little for that extra note to balance the flavours.

Herbs

Fresh herbs are essential in good cooking and add so much to a dish, making it taste bright and abundantly fragrant. Supermarkets now stock a wide range of fresh herbs, so all of these should be easy to find. Avoid dried herbs that have sat on the shelf too long and have gone stale. Better still is to grow your own. Even the tiniest windowsill could hold a pot or two. Here are a selection of fresh herbs I couldn't do without:

* basil
* bay leaves
* coriander
* marjoram

* mint
* oregano
* parsley
* rosemary

* sage
* thyme

Stock

It's always worth having chicken stock in the freezer. If I've jointed a chicken or roasted a whole bird, I use the carcass to make my own. Home-made stocks always taste the best and they're easy to make (see *Basics*, page 225). But if you are buying it, always choose the highest quality fresh stock you can find.

Bread

Really good bread is becoming much easier to find. It may cost more than the average white sliced loaf, but it is a world apart. Loaves made using artisan techniques contain high-quality flours with valuable nutrients. The dough is left to rise slowly, which means less yeast is needed, resulting in better flavour. Cooking with good bread makes your food taste better, too. Whether it's for breadcrumbs, adding to soup or making summer pudding, a high-quality loaf will never go to waste. Making breadcrumbs is the perfect way to use up a stale loaf and you can keep the crumbs in a resealable bag in the freezer if you don't need them immediately.

To make breadcrumbs, first heat the oven to 180°C/350°F/Gas 4.

Remove the crust from the loaf (or keep it on if you like coarser crumbs), then tear the bread into small pieces. Arrange the bread in a thin layer on a baking tray and put it in the oven for about 20 minutes, or until they are dry and crunchy.

If you have a food processor, you can then blitz them into finer crumbs. If not, wrap the coarse crumbs in a tea towel or put them in a resealable bag and bash them with a rolling pin to break them into finer crumbs.

QUICK POTS

Simple weekday suppers that don't take long

On weekdays, after a tiring day's work or whenever there isn't lots of time to cook, these quick pot recipes offer some delicious meals that don't take too long to prepare.

It's amazing what you can cook up in a short amount of time without having to cut corners. Just choose the right ingredients and methods, and you can have something utterly delicious ready in no time at all.

There are warming and comforting soups like autumn squash and chestnut or lighter, fresher dishes like the spring risotto with asparagus, peas and herbs. For something more substantial, you could make white fish, steamed over Moroccan spiced vegetables, or chicken thighs roasted with lemony new potatoes. All of these are dishes that celebrate the seasons and make convenient yet satisfying dinners.

One-pot meals are perfect when you need to be quick. Not only can the ingredients all be cooked together, creating a delicious balance of flavours, but you can serve it as one complete dish too, right out of the pot, massively reducing that ever-mounting pile of washing up!

MIDDLE EASTERN AUBERGINE *and* CHICKPEAS

Serves 2

3 tbsp olive oil

1 medium aubergine, cut into 2cm-sized cubes

1 red onion, finely chopped

3 garlic cloves, finely chopped

1 red chilli, deseeded and finely chopped

1 tsp ground allspice

1 tsp ground cinnamon

1 tsp ground cumin

1 tsp smoked paprika

3 or 4 fresh tomatoes or 1 tin (400g) tomatoes, chopped

1 tin (400g) chickpeas, rinsed and drained

20g mixture of flat-leaf parsley and coriander, roughly chopped

yoghurt, to serve

salt and freshly ground black pepper

Spicy and comforting, this is one of my favourite weekday suppers. The aubergines are fried at a fairly high heat with quite a lot of oil until they become caramelised and sweet. This dish is a perfect accompaniment to grilled lamb chops but there is also enough to eat on its own with just some flat bread.

Heat the oil in a heavy-based pan with a lid on a high heat. Make sure the oil is really hot before you add the aubergines to prevent too much sticking. Fry the aubergine quickly, stirring often, so that they brown evenly all over.

Add the onion and a good pinch of salt. Turn down the heat and cook slowly for 10–15 minutes, or until the onion softens. The softening of the onion will form the flavoursome base so don't be tempted to rush this stage. Add the garlic and chilli and cook for a further minute, so that it begins to brown. Add the spices and stir well to coat.

Stir in the tomatoes to bring everything together. Continue cooking, covered over a gentle heat until the tomatoes collapse and break down into a sauce. After about 10 minutes, add the chickpeas. Continue cooking, covered, stirring occasionally for about 15 minutes, or until all the flavours blend into each other. Taste and add more salt and pepper if necessary.

Finally, stir in the parsley and coriander and allow to sit for a few minutes before serving.

Eat with hot flat breads and a spoonful of cumin and coriander yoghurt or tahini yoghurt (see pages 224–225).

FRAGRANT *and* WARMING THAI NOODLE BROTH

Serves 2

1 litre chicken stock

1 red Thai chilli, or 2 hot fresh red chillies

20g bunch of coriander, stalks and leaves roughly chopped, plus a small bunch of chopped coriander leaves, reserved

2 lime leaves

20g ginger, peeled and sliced

2 lemongrass stalks, cut into small pieces

2 tbsp Tom Yum paste

1 tbsp fish sauce, or to taste

juice of 1 lime

2 pak choi, or about 100g chard leaves

100g dried rice noodles

100g mushrooms, thinly sliced

3 tbsp tinned water chestnuts, drained

salt and freshly ground black pepper

This broth has the classic Thai flavours of lemongrass, ginger, coriander and lime leaves, and it's very straightforward to make. Many of these ingredients can be kept in the store cupboard or freezer so this healthy, tasty soup can be thrown together at the very last minute.

Add the chicken stock, the chillies, coriander stalks, lime leaves, ginger, lemongrass and Tom Yum paste to a large saucepan over a medium heat. Bring to a simmer.

Continue to simmer for 10 minutes, then strain and discard the flavourings. Return the aromatic broth to the saucepan and bring back to a simmer.

Add the fish sauce and lime juice to taste. The flavour should be slightly sweet and fragrant, salty from the fish sauce, hot from the chilli and sour from the lime.

Meanwhile, strip the leaves of the pak choi or chard (if using) from its stems and tear any larger leaves in half. Chop the stems into small pieces and set aside.

Put the rice noodles in a bowl and pour over enough boiling water (I use water from the kettle) to cover. Soak for 2 minutes, then drain.

Add the drained noodles to the broth, then the mushrooms and water chestnuts and cook together for a couple of minutes.

Divide the noodles and vegetables between bowls. Pour the steaming hot broth poured over the top, sprinkle with the reserved chopped coriander leaves and serve.

LIGHT SUMMER
SOUP *with* PISTOU

Serves 4

2 tbsp olive oil

I medium red
onion, diced

2 garlic cloves,
finely sliced

2 large courgettes,
quartered lengthways and
thickly sliced

300g green beans,
topped and tailed and
cut into 2cm lengths

150g fresh peas, shelled
(or frozen, if necessary)

I litre water

salt and freshly ground
black pepper

For the pistou

I garlic clove

small pinch of salt

40g pine nuts

80g basil, roughly chopped

90ml olive oil

This Provençale soup can be made with any selection of vegetables that are in season. As a winter alternative you could easily use haricot beans, carrots or turnips. The key to its flavour is to cook the vegetables for a long time before adding the water to draw out their sweetness. 'Pistou', which comes from the French word meaning 'to pound', is similar to Italian pesto, but without the cheese.

In a large, heavy-based pan with a lid, heat the oil over a low heat. Add the onion along with a pinch of salt and fry for 10 minutes or until soft, golden and sweet. Add the garlic and continue to cook for another couple of minutes, then add the courgettes.

Stir well, cover and cook gently for 10–15 minutes, stirring occasionally to prevent the vegetables from sticking to the bottom of the pan.

When the courgettes are really soft and sweet-tasting, add the beans and continue to cook for another 5 minutes. Finally add the peas and cover with the water. Season well and simmer for about 10 minutes, or until the beans are soft.

Meanwhile, prepare the pistou. Pound the garlic to a paste with salt, ideally in a pestle and mortar. Then add the pine nuts and basil and crush to make a thick green paste. Pour in the oil and mix together to loosen.

Serve the soup with a spoonful of pistou in the middle and stir through.

RISOTTO *with* ASPARAGUS, PEAS *and* LEMON

Serves 4

40g unsalted butter

1 red onion, finely diced

200g risotto rice

100ml white wine

1 litre hot chicken stock

300g asparagus, cut into short lengths

300g peas, podded

20g bunch each of mint, parsley, basil and oregano, chopped

zest of ½ lemon

25g Parmesan

salt and freshly ground black pepper

This is one of the most freshly flavoured risottos to cook in spring or early summer, when asparagus and peas come into season. Always use the freshest vegetables you can find. Broad beans, courgettes and baby artichokes are all delicious alternatives.

In a heavy-based pan, melt half of the butter over a medium heat. Add the onion and a little salt and fry gently for 5–10 minutes, or until it is soft and sweet but not coloured. Add the rice and stir well to coat the rice in the butter.

Pour in the wine so that it all sizzles and allow it to bubble for a couple of minutes, stirring until the liquid is almost completely absorbed. Then add a ladleful of stock, stirring occasionally until it is almost all absorbed before you add the next one. After the first couple of ladles, add the asparagus and season everything well.

Keep adding stock (a ladleful at a time) and stir. After 10 minutes or so, once the asparagus starts to become tender, add the peas. After 15–20 minutes, depending on the heat and the size of your pot, the risotto will look creamy but the rice will still have a little bite, without feeling chalky inside. It doesn't matter if you haven't added all the stock, but it's important the rice has the right creamy consistency – not too wet but not stodgy, either.

Turn off the heat and add the herbs and lemon zest, the rest of the butter, grate over the Parmesan and stir well. Check the seasoning and leave it to sit for a minute to settle before serving.

SQUASH, CHESTNUT *and* FARRO SOUP

Serves 4–6

2 tbsp olive oil

1 red onion, finely sliced

2 garlic cloves, finely sliced

20g sage, finely chopped

500g squash, peeled and
cut into 2cm chunks

200g cooked chestnuts,
finely chopped

1 litre chicken stock
or water (or a mixture
of both)

50g farro or pearl barley,
well rinsed and drained

salt and freshly ground
black pepper

extra virgin olive
oil, to serve

This wonderfully hearty soup is best made in autumn when squash are at their very best. Try experimenting with different squash varieties — I like to use acorn or Crown Prince. Farro gives the soup an earthiness and a lovely, nutty bite but, if you prefer, you can use pearl barley instead.

Heat the oil in a large, heavy-based pot over a low heat. Add the onion along with a pinch of salt.

Gently fry the onion for about 5 minutes or until it begins to soften, but don't let it colour. Add the garlic and continue to cook gently so everything becomes soft and sweet, about 5 minutes or so.

Add the sage, squash and chestnuts along with a good pinch of salt and some pepper and stir together well. Cook for another 5 minutes, stirring occasionally so it doesn't stick.

Pour over the stock, or water, and stir. Then add the farro or pearl barley. Bring to the boil and then turn down to a simmer and cook for 20 minutes, or until the squash is very soft and the farro still has a little bite to it.

Using a potato masher, gently crush the pieces to make a smoother soup, but leave a few whole parts of squash to give it a bit of bite (you can also do this with a stick blender). Test the seasoning and serve with extra virgin olive oil poured on top.

SPICED BRASSICAS *and* CHICKPEAS

Serves 4–6

600g in total of:
purple sprouting broccoli;
cauliflower; romanesco
broccoli; kale; cabbage

2 tbsp olive oil

2 shallots, sliced

3 garlic cloves, sliced

1cm piece ginger, peeled
and finely chopped

1 red chilli, deseeded and
finely chopped

1 tsp cumin seeds

1 tsp nigella seeds

1 tsp mustard seed

1 tin (400g) chickpeas,
rinsed and drained

salt and freshly ground
black pepper

To serve

2 tbsp coriander leaves,
roughly chopped

extra virgin olive oil

Greek yoghurt

A vibrant and lightly spiced winter dish, the chickpeas make this particularly substantial, but you could also serve it as a side with grilled chicken, which it goes very well with. You can choose whichever brassicas take your fancy, but I always love the beautiful fractal shapes of romanesco.

First, prepare the vegetables. Remove the tough outer leaves from the broccoli and break off the stems so that you're left with a number of small florets. Break the cauliflower and romanesco into small florets. Discard the thick stem from the kale and cabbage, and chop the leaves roughly.

Fill a large casserole or heavy-based pan with salted water and bring it to the boil. Blanch the vegetables for a couple of minutes each in the boiling water. When they are just tender, remove and set aside.

Drain the water from the pan, then return the pan to the heat with the oil. Reduce the heat to medium and fry the shallots with a pinch of salt until soft and sweet. This will take 5–10 minutes.

Add the garlic, ginger and chilli and continue to cook for 5 minutes. Sprinkle in the spices and listen to them start to crackle and pop, an indication that they are releasing their flavour.

Add the chickpeas and let them cook with the spices for 5 minutes or so, to absorb their flavour.

Add the drained vegetables and 2 tablespoons of water. Season generously with salt and pepper and stir well. Cook together for a couple of minutes to allow the vegetables to absorb the flavour of the spices. Stir in the coriander and some extra virgin olive oil. Serve with a big spoonful of Greek yoghurt on top.

COURGETTE *and* HERB FRITTATA

Serves 2

15g unsalted butter

4 spring onions,
finely sliced

1 medium courgette,
sliced

a handful of mixed herbs
(parsley, coriander, dill
and mint), chopped

½ tsp ground allspice

100g feta, crumbled

6 eggs

salt and freshly ground
black pepper

A frittata is a like a baked Italian omelette, which puffs up during cooking like a cake. It's incredibly simple to make, and using this method, you can alter the ingredients as you choose. Spinach and ricotta or asparagus and herbs are two of my other favourites.

Preheat the grill to a medium setting.

In a small, ovenproof saucepan, melt the butter over a medium heat. Add the spring onions along with a pinch of salt and sweat gently until they soften slighty. This will take a couple of minutes.

Add the courgettes and continue to cook gently for 5–10 minutes, allowing them to brown slightly and soften.

Put the herbs in a bowl with the onions, courgettes, allspice and feta. Crack in the eggs and beat very lightly, keeping parts of the egg white and yolk separate. Season well.

Pour the mixture into the pan and cook for about 4 minutes over a medium heat or until the bottom has set and browned slightly. Then put the pan under the grill for about 12 minutes. The frittata will puff up and turn a golden brown but should still be a little runny inside when cut open.

BRAISED SPRING VEGETABLES *with* PEARL BARLEY

Serves 3–4

1 medium-sized bunch asparagus (250g)

4 whole baby artichokes or 1 tin (400g) artichoke hearts, quartered

1 lemon, zest and juice

100g pearl barley or farro

2 tbsp olive oil

2 shallots, finely diced

300g fresh peas, podded

300g fresh broad beans, podded

4 slices of prosciutto

20g mint leaves, chopped

extra virgin olive oil

salt and freshly ground black pepper

Bursting with young, tender and sweet peas and broad beans cooked together with fresh-tasting mint and zesty lemon, this dish is like a celebration of spring. Leave out the prosciutto for a vegetarian alternative.

Snap off and discard the woody ends of the asparagus and chop them into short lengths.

If using fresh artichokes, boil them whole in salted water for 10 minutes, or until they are just soft in the middle. Remove and drain. Once the artichokes are cool enough to handle, peel off the tough outer leaves and trim the stalk. Baby artichokes should not have formed a choke, but if there is one, remove it with a teaspoon. Then cut the artichokes into quarters, sprinkle with lemon juice and set aside.

Fill a pan with salted water and bring to the boil. Cook the pearl barley, or farro, over a medium heat for 10–12 minutes, or until it is soft but still has some bite. Drain and set aside.

In the same pan, heat the oil over a low heat and fry the shallots slowly for 5–10 minutes, or until they are soft and sweet.

Add the peas, broad beans, artichokes and the asparagus and season well. Fry everything together for a few minutes, then add enough water to come about halfway up the vegetables. Arrange the prosciutto slices on top. Let this braise gently for about 10 minutes, so that the vegetables are soft and the flavour of the prosciutto has infused the liquid.

Lift off the layer of prosciutto and chop finely, then return it to the pan with the cooked pearl barley, lemon zest, and some of the juice, the chopped mint and olive oil.

This is best served at room temperature and tastes even better if it has been allowed to sit for a while.

STEAMED MUSSELS *and* CLAMS *with* FRESH TOMATO

Serves 4

1 tbsp olive oil

4 garlic cloves, finely chopped

2 tomatoes, cut into small pieces

1 red chilli, deseeded and finely chopped

20g flat-leaf parsley, chopped

200ml white wine

1kg mussels

500g clams

salt and freshly ground black pepper

This is the traditional method for steaming open mussels and clams, but here I've used lighter ingredients like the tomato instead of cream to keep it fresh. Ready in minutes and served straight from the pot — this dish couldn't be easier.

Prepare the shellfish. Throw away any shells that are open, broken or won't close if given a sharp tap against a bench top. Wash them in cold water, removing the beard from the mussels (the fibrous clinging tuft of hair attached to the shell).

In a large, heavy-based pan with a lid, heat the oil over a medium heat. Add the garlic and gently fry until it is just beginning to brown. Add the tomatoes, chilli and parsley and cook together for 2–3 minutes. Season with salt and pepper.

Turn up the heat and add the wine. Cook for 5 minutes to break down the tomatoes and reduce some of the liquid, then add the shellfish. Cover with the lid and cook for 5 minutes, or until all the shells have opened.

Serve with slices of good buttered bread and a salad, if you like.

MOROCCAN SPICED FISH *with* PEPPERS *and* POTATOES

Serves 2

2 tbsp olive oil

a small bunch of spring onions, finely sliced

3 garlic cloves, sliced

1 tsp ground cumin

1 tsp smoked paprika

500g potatoes, peeled and sliced

300g green pepper, deseeded and sliced

500g tomatoes, white core removed and chopped

1 tbsp black or green olives, pitted

20g coriander leaves, roughly chopped

20g flat-leaf parsley, roughly chopped

2 halibut or hake steaks (about 200g each)

1 lemon, cut into wedges

salt and freshly ground black pepper

In this dish, the flavour of Moroccan spices steam into the fish as it cooks. I prefer to use fish on the bone because it holds together well, but you could try using thick fillets of sea bass, bream, or any firm white fish as an alternative.

Heat the oil over a low heat in a large heavy-based pan with a lid. Add the spring onions along with a good pinch of salt and cook gently for 4–5 minutes or until they begin to soften. Add the garlic, cumin and paprika and continue to cook for a further couple of minutes to lightly fry the spices.

Add the sliced potatoes, season and stir well. Let the potatoes cook for a while so they start to brown and then add the green peppers and tomatoes. Stir well and cover with the lid. Cook for 10–15 minutes or until the peppers and potatoes soften and the tomatoes collapse to form a sauce.

When the vegetable are cooked and tender, stir in the olives and herbs. Put the fish on top of the vegetables and replace the lid. Turn the heat to medium and steam for about 10 minutes.

Remove the lid and check that the fish is cooked by inserting a skewer into the middle. If it slides through with no resistance it is cooked. Squeeze over the lemon wedges to serve.

MACKEREL *with* COURGETTES *and* CHILLI

Serves 4

1 small onion, finely sliced

2 medium courgettes, cut into small pieces

1 red chilli, deseeded and finely chopped

25g pine nuts

4 whole mackerel (about 200g each) gutted and cleaned

2 lemons

20g flat-leaf parsley, finely chopped

2 garlic cloves, finely chopped

1 tbsp good-quality red wine vinegar

2 tbsp olive oil

salt and freshly ground black pepper

extra lemon, for serving

Abundant and inexpensive, mackerel is a great choice of fish. Its rich, juicy flesh goes beautifully with chilli, lemon and herbs. Ask your fishmonger to gut and clean it for you if you're not sure how.

Preheat the oven to 170°C/350°F/Gas 3½.

In a large roasting tray add the onion, courgettes, chilli and pine nuts.

Season the mackerel inside their bellies and lay them on top of the courgettes, then make 3 or 4 shallow slits through their skin.

Grate the zest of both lemons, squeeze the juice from one and reserve.

Mix together the parsley, garlic and lemon zest and sprinkle over the fish, rubbing it into the skin. Add the lemon juice, vinegar and oil and season well. Mix everything together, spreading it out over the base of the roasting tray.

Bake in the oven for 30–40 minutes. Remove the fish from the oven and check if it is cooked by inserting a skewer just behind the head. It should pierce through with no resistance.

Serve with extra lemon wedges for squeezing.

CHICKEN *with* NEW POTATOES *and* LEMON

Serves 4

2 tbsp olive oil

4 chicken thighs

500g new potatoes or cut larger variety potatoes into small pieces

1 lemon, sliced into thin rounds

2 tsp capers, rinsed

1 shallot, finely sliced

10g rosemary leaves, chopped

salt and freshly ground black pepper

The lemon gives this dish a really juicy freshness. Try to use small potatoes that you can leave whole — they will cook in the same length of time as the chicken.

Preheat the oven to 200°C/400°F/Gas 6.

Place a heavy-based ovenproof pan over medium heat and add the oil. When the pan is hot, add the chicken pieces and brown all over and season well. Remove to a plate.

Add the potatoes to the pan with the lemon, capers, shallot and rosemary. Toss together and season well. Arrange the chicken pieces, skin side up, in between the potatoes so they sit nice and snug in the pan. Place the pan in the oven and roast for 30–40 minutes.

Serve with just a green salad.

RADICCHIO, RED WINE *and* PANCETTA RISOTTO

Serves 4

25g butter, plus an
extra knob

I red onion,
very finely chopped

20g rosemary, leaves
picked and roughly
chopped

70g pancetta, diced

200g risotto rice

150ml red wine

I litre hot chicken stock

200g radicchio,
thinly sliced

70g Parmesan, grated

salt and freshly ground
black pepper

Risottos don't take as long as you might think, and make perfect weekday suppers. Stirring is important but isn't necessary all the time — the rice has to be allowed to cook undisturbed, too. Adding hot stock helps the rice cook faster. I like to heat the stock in a saucepan first, pour it into a jug and keep it warm by the stove.

Place a heavy-based saucepan over a medium heat and add the butter. When it has melted, add the onion and fry until soft and sweet. This should take about 10 minutes. Add the rosemary and pancetta and cook until the pancetta begins colour and get crisp. Now add the rice and stir well to coat completely in the butter and allow it to fry for a minute or so. Add a good pinch of salt, then pour in the wine. Let it bubble well, and become almost completely absorbed, then add a ladle of hot stock. Stir a few times and allow the stock to be absorbed before adding the next ladle. Continue cooking in this way, over a low heat, until the rice is still firm on the inside but beginning to soften. This should take about 20 minutes.

Stir in the radicchio and a ladleful of stock and cook until the leaves start to wilt and turn the colour of the sauce around the rice red.

When the rice is nearly cooked but still has a little bite, add just enough stock to loosen the risotto. But don't add too much, otherwise it will become watery. Stir in the extra knob of butter, Parmesan and season well. Stir, then leave for a minute or so for the flavours to develop.

Spoon onto plates straight from the pot; the risotto should be loose enough to move slightly when it touches the plate, with a little liquid seeping out.

PORK CHOPS *with* APPLE *and* FENNEL

Serves 2

a knob of butter

2 tbsp oil

2 pork chops, weighing 400g in total

200g fennel, thinly sliced

200g apples (Cox, Russett), peeled, cored and cut into wedges

a few sprigs of thyme, leaves picked from the stalk

2 tbsp single cream

I tbsp Dijon mustard

salt and freshly ground black pepper

A very French-style dish that is rich with butter and cream but sharp with tangy apple and mustard. Good-quality pork chops with plenty of fat will ensure the meat is succulent.

Place a large, heavy-based frying pan on a fairly high heat. Add the butter and oil. When it starts to foam, put in the chops. Season well with salt and pepper and cook for about 5 minutes on each side, including the skin side, until they are nicely brown and the flesh feels firm when you press it. Transfer the chops to a plate and cover with foil to keep warm.

Turn the heat to medium and add the fennel, apple, thyme leaves and another pinch of salt. Stir well to coat everything in the remaining butter. Allow this to cook for about 5 minutes so it all begins to soften and lightly colour.

Add the cream, mustard and about 100ml of water and continue to cook for a further few minutes, or until the fennel and apple have become soft and slightly brown and a sauce is forming. Return the chops to the pan, along with any of their juices.

Serve straight from the pan with the fennel, apple and juices spooned over and mustard on the table.

SAUSAGES *and* BEANS

Serves 2

2 tbsp olive oil

250g pork sausages
(or 2 large sausages)

I red onion, finely sliced

10g rosemary leaves

I tin (400g) tomatoes

2 bay leaves

I tbsp red wine vinegar

I tbsp molasses

½ tsp dried chilli flakes

I tsp smoked paprika

I tin (400g) borlotti beans

salt and freshly ground
black pepper

This home-made version of baked beans, cooked together with sausages, makes a meal in itself. This dish is just as good eaten for breakfast on toast as it is the next day. I like to use Toulouse sausages made with herbs, garlic and wine because they have a great taste, but you can also use your own favourites.

In a large, heavy-based pan with a lid, heat the oil over a medium heat. When the oil is hot, add the sausages and brown them all over, then remove to a plate and set aside.

Add the onion to the pan with a good pinch of salt and cook to soften slightly. Add the rosemary, tomatoes and bay leaves and cook together for about 5 minutes. Then add the rest of the ingredients and stir well. Return the browned sausages to the pan. Check for seasoning and then turn the heat down. Partially cover with the lid and allow to simmer gently for about 30 minutes, stirring occasionally, until you have a thick sauce. If it looks like it's getting a bit dry, stir in a little water to keep a good consistency.

SLOW POTS

Comforting weekend dishes that you can spend more time on

This is the kind of cooking to do when you're not in a rush, when the preparation can be as much a part of the enjoyment as the eating.

These are dishes that can be cooked gently for several hours, soups that gain all their flavour from the long cooking of their base vegetables, and other simple dishes that benefit from a little time putting them together.

These recipes are based on the classic methods of slow cooking often using inexpensive cuts of meat that become unctuous and tender when given plenty of time, bringing out the best of their character. The beef in the pot-au-feu is cooked over several hours and absorbs the flavour of the surrounding vegetables while braising in a delicious broth. In the winter minestrone, all of the flavour comes from the slow caramelisation of the vegetables at the beginning of cooking. This method gently extracts the sweetness of the vegetables and can also be used to make the perfect base for a fish stew or a long-cooked tomato sauce.

Here is weekend cooking at its best. Take the time to relish the things involved in assembling a dish, whether it's rolling meatballs, rubbing in spices or stuffing courgettes.

Slow pot recipes might require a little time to prepare but then you can leave them to cook while you do something else. Don't rush, enjoy being in the kitchen — and take pleasure in transforming your ingredients into something really special.

WINTER MINESTRONE
with PASTA *and* BEANS

Serves 6–8

2 tbsp olive oil

2 large carrots, peeled and diced

I red onion, finely diced

3 celery stalks, finely diced

3 garlic cloves, sliced

20g flat-leaf parsley, roughly chopped

a couple of sprigs of marjoram, roughly chopped

I tin (400g) tomatoes

300g cavolo nero, or Russian kale, stalks removed, roughly chopped

I tin (400g) cooked borlotti beans, rinsed and drained

1.5 litres cold water

100g dried spaghetti, broken into pieces or small minestrone pasta

salt and freshly ground black pepper

To serve

Parmesan

extra virgin olive oil

All the flavour of this soup comes from the slow cooking of the soffritto, the base vegetables. The longer you cook this, the sweeter the flavour, and you need only add water not stock. I love using Russian kale, which is very tender and takes less time to cook but you can use any leafy green available.

In a large, heavy-based saucepan, heat the olive oil over a low heat. Add the carrots, onion, celery and a good pinch of salt and cook gently for 20–30 minutes, or until they are soft and just beginning to colour. Add the garlic and cook for 5 minutes. By now, the vegetables should be lightly coloured and very soft and sweet.

Turn up the heat a little and stir in the chopped herbs and fry for a couple of minutes. Add the tomatoes and stir well. Turn the heat down to low and continue to cook for a further 10 minutes, or until the tomato is well reduced. You should by now have a thick base of sweet, browned vegetables and tomato.

Add the cavolo nero (or kale) and the beans and cover with the cold water. Season with salt and pepper, stir and bring to the boil. Turn the heat down to a simmer and cook, partially covered, for 10 minutes.

Add the pasta and continue to cook for a further 10 minutes, or until the pasta is al dente. Turn off the heat and leave to stand for up to 15 minutes – this will allow the flavours to develop.

Finally, check the seasoning and reheat before serving.

To serve, divide the minestrone between serving bowls, and grate the Parmesan over before drizzling in a good glug of extra virgin olive oil.

CAULIFLOWER
and POTATO CURRY

Serves 4

1 tsp coriander seeds

1 tsp mustard seeds

1 tsp fenugreek seeds

1 tsp cumin seeds

3 tbsp groundnut oil

1 large onion, finely sliced

½ tsp ground cinnamon

1 tsp ground turmeric

1 red chilli, deseeded
and finely chopped

2cm piece ginger, peeled
and finely chopped

2 garlic cloves, finely sliced

800g potatoes, peeled and
cut into 2cm pieces

200ml water

2 tomatoes,
roughly chopped

1 small head cauliflower,
broken into florets

20g fresh coriander,
roughly chopped

salt and freshly ground
black pepper

Fragrant, colourful and wonderfully filling, this vegetable curry is heady with spice and is so comforting and healthy too. It's also really simple to prepare. If you have a pestle and mortar, this is the perfect opportunity to toast and grind the spices yourself.

Toast the coriander, mustard, fenugreek and cumin seeds in a dry heavy-based pan over a medium heat (the one you will use to cook the curry in will do fine). Don't add any oil, just fry for a minute or so until the spices begin to crackle and start to release their fragrance. Be careful not to let them burn, though.

Tip the spices into a pestle and mortar and grind well. This is the wonderful moment when all the amazing aromas are released.

Reduce the heat and add the oil. Then add the onion and a good pinch of salt. Cook for a couple of minutes, then add the ground spices, chilli, ginger and garlic. Put the lid on and cook on a gentle heat for at least 5 minutes, or until everything begins to soften but not brown.

Add the potatoes and season well. Let them fry briefly for 2–3 minutes, then add the water and tomatoes. Cover and simmer gently for 20–30 minutes, or until the potatoes are almost soft.

Now stir in the cauliflower. Cover and let the mixture steam and cook for a further 15–20 minutes, or until the vegetables are soft but still holding together and the flavour of the spices has been absorbed.

Remove the lid and cook uncovered for 5–10 minutes. Sprinkle with the coriander and serve with a cooling cucumber raita (see page 224), naan bread or steamed rice.

FISH STEW

Serves 4

2 tbsp olive oil

4 garlic cloves, finely sliced

1½ tsp fennel seeds, crushed roughly

2 red chillies, deseeded and finely chopped

400g fennel, sliced

150ml white wine

900g tomatoes, white core removed, roughly chopped

1 large pinch of saffron

20g flat-leaf parsley, roughly chopped

400g small, waxy potatoes, peeled

800g white fish fillets such as sea bass or hake, skin removed, cubed

600g mussels or clams or a mixture of both

salt and freshly ground black pepper

This dish is inspired by the simplicity of Italian fish stews where all the flavour comes from the freshest ingredients. You won't need a complicated stock for this recipe. The base can be prepared in advance, with the fish cooked just before serving. Use a pot large enough to accommodate everything, and then bring it to the table for everyone to help themselves.

First, prepare the shellfish. Throw away any shells that are open, broken or won't close if given a sharp tap against a bench top. Wash the mussels and clams in cold water, removing the beard from the mussels (the fibrous, clinging tuft of hair attached to the shell).

In a large, heavy-based pan with a lid, heat the oil over a medium heat and fry the garlic until it is just starting to brown. Add the fennel seeds and chillies and season well. Now add the sliced fennel and a good pinch of salt and cook for a few minutes to soften.

Pour over the wine and allow it to bubble and reduce slightly, then add the tomatoes and saffron. Stir well, then add the parsley and season generously with salt and pepper. Add the potatoes and cover with water. Simmer for 20 minutes, or until the potatoes are tender.

Now add the fish and shellfish and stir gently to cover with sauce. Cover and cook at a gentle boil for about 10 minutes, or until the clams and mussels are open and the fish pieces are cooked through.

Serve immediately divided in shallow bowls alongside toasted bread rubbed with garlic and olive oil.

BAKED AUBERGINE *with* MOZZARELLA, TOMATO *and* COURGETTE

Serves 4

1 medium aubergine, sliced into rounds 5mm thick

2 medium courgettes, sliced into rounds 5mm thick

400g tomatoes, sliced into 5mm rounds

4 garlic cloves, crushed to a paste with salt

1 tsp thyme leaves, chopped

3 tbsp olive oil

220g buffalo mozzarella, sliced

20g Parmesan

40g white breadcrumbs

salt and freshly ground black pepper

A very rich and delicious vegetarian dish, oozing with mozzarella. The secret is to allow it plenty of cooking time so the vegetables become really soft and the breadcrumbs on top golden and crunchy.

Preheat the oven to 180°C/350°F/Gas 4.

In a bowl, mix the sliced aubergine, courgettes, tomatoes and salt and pepper with the crushed garlic, thyme and olive oil. (Don't worry if the tomatoes break up; they are there to provide the juiciness.)

Arrange the aubergine slices in a layer in a large baking dish. Cover with a layer of mozzarella followed by a layer of tomatoes and courgettes. Scrape any garlic and thyme left in the bowl over the top.

Sprinkle the Parmesan and breadcrumbs evenly on top and loosely cover with foil, shiny-side down. (Covering with foil shiny-side down will reflect the heat back into the dish.) Bake for about 50 minutes and remove the foil. Return to the oven and cook for another 5–10 minutes, or until the top is golden brown and crunchy.

Serve with a green salad.

POACHED CHICKEN
with SALSA VERDE

Serves 4

2 bay leaves

a small bunch each of
thyme and
parsley stalks

1.5kg whole chicken

300g new potatoes, peeled

300g carrots, peeled
and left whole

6 garlic cloves, peeled

400g leeks, sliced into
4cm lengths

2 celery stalks, halved

½ tsp freshly ground
black pepper

1 tsp salt

250g spinach (optional)

For the salsa verde

6 anchovy fillets,
finely chopped

3 tsp capers, rinsed and
finely chopped

150g chopped mixed
herbs (parsley, mint,
oregano, basil)

1 tsp Dijon mustard

1 tsp red wine vinegar

90–120ml extra
virgin olive oil

*A simple, healthy dish that also leaves you with extra chicken stock,
which will be useful for making risottos or soup another time.
Salsa verde is a vibrantly green, herbed sauce seasoned with capers,
anchovies and mustard. It is perfect served alongside meat or fish.*

Tie the herbs in a bundle and set aside.

Put the chicken in a large pot over a medium heat and cover with water.
Bring to a simmer, skimming off any scum that rises to the surface and
topping up with cold water as necessary. Once all the scum has risen
to the surface and has been removed, add the potatoes, carrots, garlic,
leeks, celery, herb bundle, pepper and salt. Cover and simmer for
50 minutes.

Meanwhile, prepare the salsa verde in a bowl. Mix all the ingredients
together to make a thick green sauce. Set aside.

Remove the chicken from the pot. Insert a skewer into the leg and if the
juices run clear the chicken is done. Remove the herb bundle and the
leeks from the pot using a slotted spoon and discard. Taste the stock and
season if necessary.

Add the spinach leaves (if using) to the stock and continue to cook for a
minute, or until they are well wilted.

To serve, carve the chicken into joints. Divide the chicken between
serving dishes and add some poached vegetables and a spoonful of stock
to each. Place a dollop of salsa verde on top.

Any leftover stock can be put in the fridge for up to 2 days or will freeze
well for up to a month.

CHICKEN TAGINE *with* PRESERVED LEMON, POTATO *and* OLIVES

Serves 4

2 tsp ground turmeric

2 tsp ground ginger

2 tsp ground cinnamon

a pinch of saffron

1.5kg chicken, jointed

4 tbsp olive oil

2 medium onions, peeled and grated

40g coriander, leaves and stalks washed

600g waxy potatoes, or Jerusalem artichokes, peeled and sliced into 2cm strips

3 preserved lemons, flesh removed and pith sliced, or 1 fresh lemon, sliced into thin rounds

100g green olives, rinsed

salt and freshly ground black pepper

A tagine is such an elegant one-pot dish and it's so straightforward to prepare. If you don't have a tagine, any good, low-sided pot with a lid will do just fine.

Mix the turmeric, ground ginger, cinnamon and saffron together in a large bowl. Add the chicken pieces and toss to coat. Season well.

Heat the oil in the tagine or pot. Add the chicken pieces and brown all over. Add the onions and half of the coriander and cook together for a couple of minutes. Pour over about 250ml water (this may vary depending on your pan, but you should have just enough water to almost cover the chicken). Arrange the potato slices in a layer on the top. Depending on the size of your pot, this may become 2 or 3 layers. Between each layer, add the lemon and olives. If you have only one layer of potatoes, arrange the lemon slices and olives on top of this. Season well.

Put on the lid and cook slowly for 30 minutes, or until the potatoes are soft. Remove the lid and continue cooking to allow the liquid to reduce by about half.

To serve, sprinkle over the remaining coriander.

ENDIVE *and* SQUASH GRATIN

Serves 2–3

600g endives, quartered
lengthways

400g squash, peeled,
deseeded and sliced into
1cm strips

1 garlic clove, crushed to a
paste with salt

1 tbsp thyme leaves,
chopped

170ml single cream

40g white breadcrumbs

40g Gruyère or
Parmesan, grated

20g unsalted butter,
cubed

salt and freshly ground
black pepper

*This is a lovely dish to eat on its own, especially as a vegetarian option.
You could also serve it as a side dish to accompany roast chicken. The
endives become juicy and soft, their slight bitterness balanced perfectly
with the sweetness of the squash. I tend to use butternut squash to
make this gratin but acorn or onion squash would work well too.*

Preheat the oven to 160°C/325°F/Gas 3.

Arrange the endives and the squash in 2 layers in a large baking dish,
and set aside.

Mix together the crushed garlic, thyme and cream. Add this to the
endives and squash and toss together well.

Season well and then sprinkle over the breadcrumbs and cheese evenly
to cover. Dot the cubes of butter over the surface and put it in the oven
to bake for 30–40 minutes.

When the top becomes golden and crunchy and the endives and squash
soft and juicy underneath the dish is ready.

Serve with a green salad dressed with a good mustardy vinaigrette.

PORK COOKED *in* MILK *with* POTATOES *and* SAGE

Serves 4

2 tbsp olive oil,
for frying

1.5kg boneless shoulder
of pork

a knob of butter

6 garlic cloves, peeled
and halved

small bunch of sage

small bunch of thyme

750ml full-fat milk

zest of 1 lemon, peeled
in long slivers

fresh nutmeg

400g potatoes, peeled
and left whole

salt and freshly ground
black pepper

Slow-cooking pork or chicken in milk is a traditional Italian method that renders the meat wonderfully succulent. The richness of this dish is balanced perfectly by the citrus of the lemon and the distinctive fresh sage. It tastes delicious with the potatoes that have been soaking in the deeply flavoured milk.

Choose a large casserole with a lid, which will comfortably hold the pork with enough space around it for the potatoes.

Preheat the oven to 160°C/325°F/Gas 3.

Place the casserole over medium heat and add the oil. Add the pork and brown on all sides. Remove the pork to a plate. Wipe all of the oil from the pan, which will have got too hot and may have burnt.

On a medium heat, melt the butter. Add the garlic, sage, thyme and cook for a minute or until the garlic is just starting to turn golden brown. Return the pork to the pan and pour over the milk. Add the slivers of lemon zest and a grating of nutmeg. Season generously with salt and pepper. Fit the potatoes around the pork so they are submerged in the milk.

Cover with a piece of baking parchment, then place the lid on top. Roast in the oven for 1½–2 hours, or until the pork is very tender and milk reduced to a creamy sauce. At this point you can remove the lemon zest if you like.

Serve hot, straight from the pot, with a green salad.

BEEF MEATBALLS *in* SPICED TOMATO SAUCE

Serves 4

500g minced beef

I tsp garam marsala

I tsp ground cumin

I tsp ground turmeric

I large onion, peeled and grated

I tbsp coriander leaves, chopped

I tbsp mint leaves, chopped

I egg

2–3 tsp each sea salt and freshly ground black pepper

3 tbsp olive oil, for frying

For the sauce

4 garlic cloves, sliced

2cm piece ginger, peeled and grated

I tsp ground allspice

I tsp ground cinnamon

½ tsp dried chilli flakes

2 tins (800g) tomatoes

salt and freshly ground black pepper

To serve

20g coriander leaves, chopped

extra virgin olive oil

The meatballs and the sauce can be made in advance separately and then heated together just before serving, allowing the sauce to sit for a few hours will improve the flavour. I also love serving this on top of spaghetti and sometimes I make it with minced lamb, which works wonderfully too.

Make the meatballs by putting all the ingredients (except the oil) in a bowl and squeezing together with your hands to make a smooth mixture. It might seem like a lot of salt and pepper to use, but this is necessary to properly season all the meat.

Form the mixture into small balls about the size of a walnut, depending on the how many you choose to make – about 20 is a good number.

In a deep, heavy frying pan, heat 2 tablespoons of oil over a medium heat and fry the meatballs, rolling them around until they brown evenly all over. You might need to fry the meatballs in batches depending on how many fit in your pan (the main thing is not to overcrowd the pan, letting the meatballs unstick before turning them over). Remove to a plate and set aside.

To make the sauce, heat the remaining I tablespoon of oil in the same frying pan over a medium heat. Add the garlic and ginger and fry for a couple of minutes so it begins to brown. Add the allspice, cinnamon and chilli flakes and stir to release the flavours. Put in the tomatoes and season well. Stir, then lower the heat and gently simmer for about 15 minutes or until you have a thick, concentrated sauce.

Add most of the coriander and stir well, then return the meatballs to the pan. Cover them in the sauce and cook together for about 5 minutes to allow the flavours to mix.

Finally, sprinkle over the rest of the coriander and serve with a drizzle of good olive oil and some good bread.

SALT BEEF *and* DUMPLINGS

Serves 4–6

1.5kg salted beef brisket or silverside

1 small onion, peeled and studded with 6 cloves

mace blade or a small piece of fresh nutmeg

8 black peppercorns

1 head of garlic, separated into unpeeled cloves

1 bunch of thyme

3 bay leaves

450g carrots, peeled

150ml red wine

250g spinach leaves, washed

For the dumplings (makes 12)

125g self-raising flour, plus extra for dusting

60g shredded suet

a pinch of salt

1 egg, beaten

4 tbsp grated horseradish

A very traditional British winter dish that is hearty and fortifying. The beef cooks very slowly in the red wine, which gives a robust, full-flavoured broth in which to poach the dumplings.

Put the beef into a large pot or casserole over a medium heat and cover with cold water. Slowly bring the water almost to the boil, then turn down to a simmer, scoop off any scum that rises to the surface. Once you have removed most of the scum, pour in a glass of cold water and repeat the process. (The cold water helps to bring any more impurities to the surface.)

Taste the water, and if it is very salty, drain and replace with clean water. If it is palatably salty, leave the beef to cook in this liquid.

Add the onion studded with cloves, mace or nutmeg, peppercorns, garlic and thyme, bay leaves, carrots and wine. Partially cover and simmer for 3 hours, topping up with water to keep everything submerged, if necessary.

Meanwhile, make the dumplings. Sift the flour into a bowl and stir in the suet and salt. Make a well in the middle and add the egg and the horseradish. Bring the mixture together, adding a tablespoon of water if necessary to form a sticky but firm dough.

With a little extra flour on your hands, pull off small pieces of the mixture and roll into walnut-sized balls. Set aside on a lightly floured baking tray.

After the beef has been cooking for about 2½ hours, remove the onion and peppercorns with a slotted spoon, leaving the carrots behind with the beef, if you like. Add the dumplings to the pot and replace the lid.

After 30 minutes, test one of the dumplings to make sure it is cooked. When the dumplings are done, remove them with a slotted spoon. Add the spinach to the broth and allow it to wilt for a couple of minutes.

Remove the beef from the broth and slice. Serve with the dumplings and a little broth, spinach and carrots.

ROASTED LOIN *of* VENISON *with* ROOT VEGETABLES

Serves 6

1.5kg rolled venison loin

1 tsp juniper berries, lightly crushed

20g rosemary leaves, roughly chopped

2 tbsp redcurrant or crab apple jelly

2 red onions, finely sliced

300ml red wine

6 garlic cloves, peeled

400g beetroot, peeled and cut into wedges

300g parsnips, cut lengthways

300g carrots, peeled and cut into lengths

400g potatoes, halved or quartered, depending on their size

3 tbsp olive oil

2 tbsp thyme, roughly chopped

60ml meat stock or water

salt and freshly ground black pepper

horseradish sauce, to serve

A perfect winter Sunday lunch to share among family and friends. The rich flavours of venison go particularly well with the sweetness of redcurrant and root vegetables. Venison is particularly good served pink and any leftovers make fantastic sandwiches with rocket and horseradish.

Marinate the venison with the juniper, rosemary, redcurrant jelly, onions and red wine overnight or for at least 4 hours.

Preheat the oven to 200°C/400°F/Gas 6.

Transfer the venison from the marinade to a large roasting tray. Season well. Strain the marinade into a jug. Reserve some of the onions and set aside for later.

In a bowl, mix the garlic, beetroot, parsnips, carrots and potatoes with the olive oil and thyme. Add them to the roasting tin around the meat and arrange the reserved onions over and around the venison.

Roast for 30 minutes, if you like it pink, or longer for well done. A good way to test for doneness is to insert a skewer through the fleshiest part of the meat and leave it for 10 seconds. Pull it out of the meat and immediately run your fingers along the skewer (don't worry, it won't be hot enough to burn you) and if it is hot at either end and just blood temperature in the middle, the meat will be pink and rare.

Then remove everything from the tin and set aside in a warm place while the meat rests for 15 minutes.

To make a light gravy, set the tin over a medium heat. Stir in the juice from the marinade and stock or water to scrape up all the caramelised residue from the bottom of the tin. Season to taste.

Slice the meat and serve with the roasted vegetables, some gravy and a dollop of horseradish sauce.

LAMB HARIRA
with CHICKPEAS

Serves 6

2 tbsp olive oil

300g neck lamb fillet,
or boneless chops or
shoulder

2 large carrots, roughly
chopped into 1cm dice

4 celery stalks, diced

4 garlic cloves, finely sliced

2 tsp ground turmeric

1 tsp ground cinnamon

2 tsp ground ginger

20g flat-leaf parsley,
roughly chopped

1 bay leaf

1 tin (400g) tomatoes

1 tbsp harissa paste or 1 red
chilli, deseeded and finely
chopped

1 tin (400g) chickpeas,
rinsed and drained

1.5 litres cold water

salt and freshly ground
black pepper

To serve

juice of ½ lemon

20g coriander
leaves, chopped

Harira is a traditional Moroccan soup in which the lamb cooks slowly in fragrant, spicy broth until it is melting and falling apart. The combination of vegetables, lamb and chickpeas makes this quite a filling soup, almost like a light stew.

In a large, heavy-based pan over a medium heat, add the oil. Add the lamb and brown well all over. Transfer to a plate and set aside.

Add the carrots and celery along with a pinch of salt to the pan. Fry for a minute or so until they begin to soften, then add the garlic, turmeric, cinnamon, ginger, parsley and bay. Stir well and cook together for a couple of minutes – a wonderful aroma of spices and herbs will rise from the pan. Stir in the tomatoes and harissa (or chilli) and let it simmer for a few minutes, then add the chickpeas. Season generously with salt and pepper and return the browned lamb to the pan. Cover with the water, stir and bring to a simmer. Cook for 2½–3 hours, partially covered, skimming occasionally if any bubbly scum rises to the surface.

After this time, you can turn off the heat and let it sit to cool completely, allowing the flavours to develop further. When the lamb is cool enough to handle, remove it from the pot. Tear or cut the lamb into bite-sized pieces and return it to the pot.

Heat to a simmer to warm the lamb through. To serve, sprinkle over the lemon juice and coriander.

COURGETTES STUFFED
with SPICED LAMB

Serves 4

4 medium courgettes

300g minced lamb

1 small onion, grated

1 tomato, diced

10g mint, chopped

1 tsp ground cumin

½ tsp ground cinnamon

½ tsp dried chilli flakes

10g pine nuts

2 tbsp olive oil

salt and freshly ground
black pepper

For the mint yoghurt

6 tbsp yoghurt

1 small tomato, finely
chopped

10g mint, finely chopped

salt and freshly ground
black pepper

A dish inspired by the cuisine of the Middle East, full of spicy flavour and balanced with a cooling mint yoghurt. Don't be put off by the thought of stuffing the courgettes, it's incredibly easy to scoop out the seeds and spoon in the stuffing.

Preheat the oven to 180°C/350°F/Gas 4.

Slice the courgettes in half lengthways and scoop out the seeds.

Mix the lamb, onion, tomato, mint, spices and pine nuts together in a bowl. Season very well – the lamb will take about 1½ teaspoons of salt.

Spoon the lamb mixture into the prepared courgettes and fit them snugly into a large baking dish. Pour over the oil.

Bake for 40 minutes or until the lamb is browned on top and the courgettes are soft.

To prepare the mint yoghurt, in a bowl, mix together the yoghurt, tomato and mint and season well.

Serve the stuffed courgettes with the mint yoghurt spooned over the top or on the side.

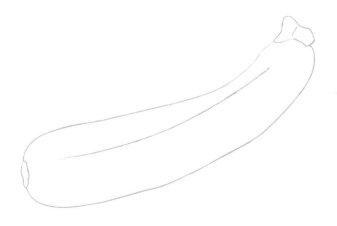

LAMB SHANKS *with* PEAS *and* GREMOLATA

Serves 4 generously

4 lamb shanks

2 tbsp plain flour, seasoned with salt and pepper, for dusting

4 tbsp olive oil

4 celery stalks, finely sliced

1 red onion, diced

2 medium carrots, peeled and diced

4 garlic cloves, finely chopped

2 tbsp chopped flat-leaf parsley

100ml white wine

500ml chicken stock

300g fresh peas, podded

salt and freshly ground black pepper

For the gremolata

20g flat-leaf parsley, chopped

1 garlic clove, finely chopped

zest of 1 lemon

Gremolata is an Italian garnish made from a mixture of chopped parsley, lemon zest and garlic. Here it adds a burst of freshness to the beautifully tender, slow-cooked lamb. A single lamb shank provides a generous amount of meat, so if you prefer a lighter meal, you could share three shanks between four people.

Preheat the oven to 150°C/300°F/Gas 2.

Dust the lamb shanks in the flour.

In a large, heavy-based pan with a lid, heat the oil over a medium heat. Add the lamb and brown all over. Remove to a plate and set aside.

In the same pan, fry the celery, onion and carrots with a good pinch of salt, for at least 5–10 minutes so it begins to colour and become soft and sweet. Add the garlic and parsley and continue to cook for a few more minutes, then pour over the wine. Let it bubble and boil for a minute or so, then return the lamb shanks to the pan. Pour over the stock. Bring it to the boil and turn it down to a simmer.

Cover with a layer of baking parchment and the lid. Roast in the oven for at least 1½ hours, or until the meat is falling off the bone.

In the meantime, prepare the gremolata. Mix the chopped parsley with the garlic and grate over the lemon zest. Chop everything together to mix it well and set aside.

After 1 hour of cooking, remove the lamb from the oven and add the peas. If there is a lot of liquid, return to the oven without the lid, otherwise continue to cook as before for another 30 minutes.

When the peas and lamb are soft, remove it from the pot. Taste the sauce for seasoning. If it is still very liquid, place the pot over a high heat and boil until the sauce is reduced to your desired consistency.

Serve the lamb and peas together with lots of the cooking sauce and the gremolata sprinkled over the top.

BRAISED LAMB SHOULDER *with* TURNIPS

Serves 4–6

800g turnips

2 tbsp olive oil

1.5–2kg lamb shoulder

2 medium onions, sliced

20g thyme leaves, picked
from the stalk

20g rosemary, picked
from the stalk

150ml white wine

150ml chicken stock

salt and freshly ground
black pepper

Lamb and turnips were made for each other: the subtle peppery taste of this vegetable stands up well to the strongly flavoured lamb. If you can buy the turnips with their leaves still attached, these taste delicious lightly wilted in the braise at the end.

Preheat the oven to 170°C/350°F/Gas 3½.

Prepare the turnips: if the skin feels very rough, peel them, and if the leaves are still attached, cut them off, rinse and set aside. Cut the turnips into quarters.

In a large roasting tin over a medium heat, add the oil. When the oil is hot, add the lamb and brown on all sides. Remove and set aside.

Add the onions to the pan, with a good pinch of salt and cook gently for at least 5 minutes, or until they begin to soften. Add the turnips and herbs and continue to cook so the turnips colour slightly.

Return the lamb to the pan and pour over the wine. Let the wine bubble for a minute or so, to burn off the alcohol, then add the chicken stock. Bring to a simmer and season well, then cover with a layer of baking parchment and foil on top and seal well. Roast for 1½–2 hours, or until the lamb is so tender it is almost falling off the bone.

If using the turnip tops with their leaves, scatter them in 20 minutes before the end of cooking to wilt in the sauce.

Remove the lamb and turnips to a plate and keep warm. Reduce the sauce by boiling if necessary. To serve, pour the sauce over the turnips and the lamb.

LITTLE POTS

Good things to make for one or two

It's good to know there are some really delicious recipes out there, ones that are worth making even if you are just preparing them for one. Little pots are all about dishes that you can throw together quickly and that bring so much pleasure in eating.

These little pots are like mini versions of quick pots: they are simple recipes that are quick to make from scratch. A favourite Sunday night supper of mine is the baked egg with spinach and blue cheese, which is cooked in 15 minutes. A tiny bit indulgent maybe, but so comforting and incredibly easy to make.

Sometimes it's nice to spend a bit more and spoil yourself. For those times we have little pots with ingredients that are slightly more expensive, like fresh crab as a sauce for linguine or spaghetti with Amalfi lemons that can be your special treat. These are dishes that use the best ingredients, simply prepared and served.

In the following pages there are great recipes to make as fuss-free starters, for instance baked peppers with mozzarella or Mexican sweetcorn soup. Or you could make the dhal or pilaf as a side dish to serve with lamb chops or grilled fish for your main.

When cooking can be this straightforward, you'll find you want to do it all the time.

MEXICAN SWEETCORN SOUP *with* CHIPOTLE

Serves 2

2 tbsp olive oil

I small onion, finely sliced

2 garlic cloves, finely
chopped

800g sweetcorn, either
cut from 4 corn cobs
or frozen, plus a few
spoonfuls whole kernels
reserved (optional)

2 tbsp chipotle paste

20g coriander, roughly
chopped

600ml water

2 tbsp crème fraîche or
soured cream

salt and freshly ground
black pepper

This soup is simple yet full of flavour: sweet, spicy and herby all at once. A dollop of something cooling like crème fraîche or soured cream offsets the heat of the chilli and adds to the creaminess. This is one of the few soups that really benefits from being blended — a stick blender does the trick perfectly, squeezing all the sweet flavour out of the corn kernels.

Choose a fairly small heavy-based saucepan with a lid. (It's easier to fry small amounts of onion in a smaller pan; they can burn quickly in a bigger pan.)

Add the oil to the pan and place over a low heat. Add the onion and a good pinch of salt and cook gently for about 10 minutes, or until it is soft, sweet and slightly coloured. Add the garlic and continue to cook for a further couple of minutes, then add the sweetcorn. Cover and cook for a further 5–10 minutes or until it starts to smell nutty and sweet.

Remove the lid and stir in the chipotle paste, most of the coriander and the water. Simmer, uncovered, for 15 minutes. Then blend well. Push as much of the mixture as you can through the sieve (I find that the back of a ladle helps with this). Not all of it will go through the sieve, but these are the rough, husky parts that you don't want to eat anyway. If you like a little texture, put in the reserved whole kernels now.

Taste for seasoning and serve with a dollop of crème fraîche or soured cream on top, sprinkled with the rest of the coriander.

AVGOLEMONO –
GREEK CHICKEN
SOUP *with* LEMON

Serves 2

I litre chicken stock

40g rice

4 eggs

juice of I lemon

20g dill or flat-leaf
parsley, chopped

salt and freshly ground
black pepper

Fresh, lemony and deeply satisfying, this is a soup that really does benefit from being made with good stock. If you've made the poached chicken with salsa verde on page 64, this is a brilliant way to make use of the leftover stock. In the summer, add broad beans if you like. Basmati and brown rice work really well, but you can use any rice you have in the cupboard.

Bring the stock to boil and add the rice. Simmer for 15–20 minutes or until the rice is soft.

In a bowl, beat the eggs with the lemon juice and chopped herbs. Whisk the eggs into the stock. The egg mixture will thicken slowly as it heats. When it has thickened, check the seasoning – the tartness of lemon often requires a little more salt to balance it – and serve.

PENNE *with* CHERRY TOMATOES *and* RICOTTA

Serves 2

200g dried penne pasta

100g cherry tomatoes, halved, or any ripe, sweet tomatoes, chopped

1 tsp red wine vinegar

1 garlic clove, crushed to a paste with a pinch of salt

1 red chilli, deseeded and finely chopped

1 tbsp extra virgin olive oil

10g basil leaves, chopped

10g oregano leaves, chopped

100g fresh ricotta

20g Parmesan, finely grated

1 handful of small rocket leaves, as peppery as possible

salt and freshly ground black pepper

The wonderful thing about this dish is that the only ingredient you need to cook is the pasta. All the other ingredients mix together to create a bright, fresh-tasting sauce. The heat from the pasta softens the tomatoes just slightly and melts the ricotta. It's the simplest summer dish to throw together and worth making, even if it's just for one.

Bring a large saucepan of salted water to the boil. Add the penne and cook for 9–12 minutes (or according to the packet instructions) until al dente.

Meanwhile, prepare the raw ingredients. Mix the cherry tomatoes with the vinegar, garlic and chilli and leave to macerate for 10 minutes.

When the pasta is cooked, drain, reserving a tablespoon of the cooking water, and quickly return both to the pan.

Add the oil, herbs, tomatoes and cheeses and mix well. Season well and finally stir in the rocket leaves.

Serve immediately.

SPAGHETTI *al* LIMONE

Serves 2

200g spaghetti

2 Amalfi or unwaxed lemons

4 tbsp extra virgin olive oil

20g flat-leaf parsley, chopped

Parmesan, grated (about 50g)

salt and freshly ground black pepper

This dish is all about simple cooking using just a few of the best ingredients you can buy. Amalfi lemons are an Italian variety that start to appear in May. These large lemons, with their fruity flavoured juice and zest, often with their leaves still attached, make this a spectacular dish. Try stirring in a couple of spoonfuls of créme fraîche and a handful of rocket leaves if you want to try a variation.

Bring a large pan of salted water to the boil. Add the spaghetti and cook for 10–12 minutes (or according to the packet instructions) until al dente.

When the pasta has cooked, drain it, keeping back a few tablespoons of the cooking liquid in the pasta (this will help everything come together). Return both to the pan.

Pour the olive oil over the pasta and mix well. Grate the zest of both lemons, then squeeze the juice over the spaghetti. Add the parsley and grated Parmesan and mix together well. Season with salt and pepper and serve.

BAKED EGGS *with* SPINACH *and* BLUE CHEESE

Serves 1 (for 2, double the quantities)

½ garlic clove

a small knob of butter

a good handful of baby-leaf spinach, shredded

2 eggs

25g mixture of blue cheese and Gruyère or Cheddar

1 tbsp single cream or crème fraîche

fresh nutmeg

salt and freshly ground black pepper

This is the ultimate Sunday night supper. Everything is easy to get hold of, and it's wonderfully quick to make. The blue cheese gives this dish incredible depth and saltiness, but if you haven't got any, of course, it's still delicious made with alternatives. A few sorrel leaves make a wonderful addition to the spinach, and Parmesan works well too — just remember to increase the quantity slightly.

Preheat the oven to 180°C/350°F/Gas 4.

Rub the inside of a ramekin or single-serving oven dish with the garlic and then with a little butter.

Put the spinach into the bottom of the dish, then break in the eggs and season well. Grate over the Gruyère and crumble in the blue cheese, then top with the cream (or crème fraîche) and a grating or so of nutmeg.

Bake for 15-20 minutes, or until the top is browned and the egg just firm.

Eat immediately if you like your yolks runny, or let it cool a little, allowing the eggs to continue to cook.

TURKISH-STYLE BAKED EGGS *with* TOMATOES

Serves 2

1 tbsp olive oil

1 small red onion, sliced

2 garlic cloves, finely sliced

1 tin (400g) tomatoes

1 tsp sugar

1 tsp cumin seeds, crushed

1 tsp smoked sweet paprika

1 tbsp chopped coriander

4 eggs

salt and freshly ground
black pepper

To serve

2 tbsp Greek yoghurt

1 tsp ground sumac

30g unsalted butter
(optional)

This warming and versatile dish is just as delicious eaten for a weekend breakfast as it is for a light dinner. The eggs cook gently in the spiced tomato sauce and to finish, just dollop over some cooling yoghurt. Serve with a good bread to mop up the sauce. The browned butter is optional — but it is really worth the extra effort!

Heat the oven to 180°C/350°F/Gas 4.

Place an ovenproof saucepan or frying pan over a medium heat. Add the oil and the onions along with a little salt and gently fry until the onion begins to soften. Add the garlic and continue to cook for a minute or so, taking care not to let them get too brown.

Add the tomatoes, sugar, cumin seeds, paprika, salt and pepper and simmer gently for 15 minutes or so, letting the sauce reduce and thicken, but stirring occasionally to prevent sticking. Finally, stir in the coriander.

Make 4 wells in the sauce with a wooden spoon and crack an egg into each. Place into the oven and bake for 5 minutes, or until the yolks are still a little soft but the whites cooked.

If making the browned butter, melt the butter in a small saucepan on a very low heat until you see little golden brown flecks on the surface of the butter (these are the milk solids beginning to caramelise and this is what gives the butter a lovely, nutty flavour). Remove immediately from the heat so it doesn't burn.

Take the eggs out of the oven and spoon onto plates. Serve with a dollop of yoghurt, a sprinkle of sumac and a drizzle of browned butter (if using) on each serving.

BAKED PEPPERS *with* MOZZARELLA *and* ANCHOVIES

Serves 2

2 sweet red peppers,
halved lengthways
and deseeded

250g buffalo mozzarella,
torn into 4 portions

8 cherry tomatoes,
halved

4 anchovy fillets

½ tsp dried chilli flakes

20g basil or marjoram
or a mixture of both,
roughly torn

2 tbsp olive oil

salt and freshly ground
black pepper

A classic Italian antipasto. Here the halved peppers provide the perfect vessel for melting mozzarella. It's a great dish to enjoy as a light lunch or supper. Feel free to vary the herbs according to what you have available or use olives instead of anchovies to get that salty flavour.

Preheat the oven to 180°C/350°F/Gas 4.

Place the peppers in a roasting tray, cut-side up and season the inside of each.

Fill each pepper half with one quarter of the mozzarella and 4 tomato halves. Then lay an anchovy fillet over the top and sprinkle over the chilli flakes and herbs. Season and drizzle over some olive oil.

Roast for 30 minutes or so until the peppers become soft and the mozzarella melts and mixes with the tomatoes and herbs.

LINGUINE *with* CRAB *and* CHILLI

Serves 2

200g linguine
or spaghetti

I garlic clove

½ tsp fennel seeds

I or 2 dressed crabs (about
250g), mixed white and
brown crabmeat

I red chilli, deseeded and
finely chopped

20g flat-leaf parsley,
chopped

juice of ½ lemon

4 tbsp extra virgin olive oil,
plus extra for serving

salt and freshly ground
black pepper

*This dish is utterly delicious and very quick to make. Paired with just
a few ingredients, the rich flavour of the crab can shine through.
Keeping some cooking water from the pasta aside and mixing it
in at the end brings everything together into a juicy sauce. This
crab mixture is also great piled onto pieces of toast that have been
rubbed with garlic and olive oil and served as an antipasto.*

Bring a large pot of salted water to the boil and add the linguine.
Cook for 8–10 minutes or according to the packet instructions.

While the pasta is cooking, use a pestle and mortar to crush the garlic
with a little salt and the fennel seeds.

In a bowl, mix the crabmeat with the garlic mixture, chilli, parsley
and lemon juice. Stir to mix and season well. Then pour over some
of the oil.

When the pasta is cooked, drain but keep 2–4 tablespoons of the
cooking water to help loosen the sauce. Return the pasta and reserved
cooking water to the pot. Stir in the crab mixture and the rest of the oil
and taste. You may want to add more lemon or oil to serve.

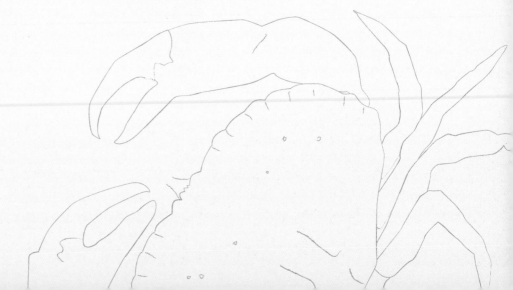

MY KIND *of* DHAL

Serves 2

200g red lentils

2 tbsp olive oil

I red onion, finely sliced

3 garlic cloves, finely sliced

I tsp ground cumin

I tsp ground turmeric

I tsp ground ginger

½ tsp ground cinnamon

I tsp nigella seeds

½ tsp dried chilli flakes

2 large tomatoes, chopped

200g spinach or
chard leaves, tough stems
removed

20g coriander,
roughly chopped

salt and freshly ground
black pepper

yoghurt, to serve (optional)

*A very simple version of dhal and one you could happily
make in less than an hour and eat as leftovers the next day.
Nearly all the ingredients can be found in the store cupboard,
ready to make a nutritious dish at a moment's notice.*

Soak the lentils in plenty of water while you prepare the rest of
the ingredients.

Heat the oil in a heavy-based pot with a lid over medium heat. Add
the onion and a pinch of salt and cook fairly quickly so that it begins
to brown. Stir in the garlic and cook until it is just starting to brown,
then add the spices. Let this cook together for a minute or so to make
an intensely fragrant base.

Add the tomatoes and another pinch of salt and let it cook for 10–15
minutes, or until reduced to a thick sauce. Meanwhile, rinse the lentils
well and drain, then add them to the tomatoes. Stir everything together
and add just enough water to cover.

Allow the lentils to simmer, covered, for about 45 minutes, or until
the lentils are tender, stirring occasionally. Add the spinach (or chard)
leaves and coriander, cover and leave for 10 minutes or until the leaves
wilt. Serve with hot naan or pitta bread and a spoonful of cucumber
raita or the cumin and coriander yoghurt (see page 224).

BROAD BEAN
and DILL PILAF

Serves 2

250g basmati rice

20g unsalted butter

1 large onion, finely diced

2 garlic cloves, sliced

1 tsp ground allspice

250g broad beans, podded

20g bunch of dill, chopped

salt and freshly ground
black pepper

This is a classic rice dish from the Middle East, where both dill and broad beans are used widely. Once you've mastered the basics of cooking pilaf, which is one of the lightest and most delicious ways to cook rice, you can alter the ingredients as you choose. This recipe also works well with peas.

Soak the rice in plenty of water with a pinch of salt while you're preparing the other ingredients.

In a heavy-based pan, melt the butter over a low heat. Add the onion along with a pinch of salt and fry gently for at least 5 minutes. Once the onions are soft and sweet, add the garlic.

Drain the rice.

Turn up the heat and add the allspice and rice to the onion mixture. Fry for a minute, stirring so that the rice is coated in the butter.

Season well and add the broad beans and dill.

Pour over enough cold water to just about 1cm over the surface and cover with a piece of baking parchment and then the lid.

Turn the heat under the pan to medium and cook for 10–15 minutes or until the rice is soft and the water absorbed. Remove from the heat and leave to sit and steam for a few minutes before serving. This pilaf is especially good served with tahini yoghurt or cucumber raita (see pages 224–225).

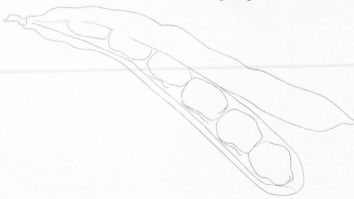

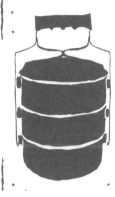

POTS TO GO

Portable food perfect for picnics or simple light lunches

These pots to go are all about quick, light lunches.
They are so much better than buying the ubiquitous
sandwich and, what's more, you can make the most
of the leftovers.

If you eat at work, there's nothing nicer than home-made food —
it's healthier, thriftier and much tastier. A salad of quinoa, chilli
and avocado, or soba noodles coated in a soy dressing, sesame and
cucumber are ideal food for a packed lunch. Grain-rich dishes such
as the barley, salted ricotta and tomato are also excellent for those
times when you feel like a light, good-for-you lunch. I tend to make
double the amount so I can enjoy eating the leftovers the next day.

Most dishes even benefit from being left until the following day
like the Tuscan tomato, basil and bread soup or the thick and
comforting courgette and white bean soup. Both of these simple
soups can be eaten at room temperature and make wonderfully
satisfying lunches.

And if you're making things to share, maybe for a picnic in the
park or an easy summer plate, a perfect portable dish could be
the Italian ragout of vegetables. On cooling the ragout becomes
juicy and deeply flavoured. All you need is some torn-up bread
to scoop it up with.

These easy yet well-balanced dishes will inspire you to eat
better, healthier food, whether you're at home, work or
just rushing around.

COURGETTE *and* WHITE BEAN SOUP

Serves 2

3 tbsp olive oil

3 garlic cloves, finely sliced

500g courgettes, trimmed and cut into chunks

400ml water or chicken stock

1 tin (400g) cannellini beans, rinsed and drained

20g basil, roughly chopped

salt and freshly ground black pepper

extra virgin olive oil, to serve

Delicious served at room temperature, this is perfect to take to work or on a picnic. The key is cooking the courgettes slowly over a low heat before adding any water, allowing them to become lovely and sweet. With a simple soup like this, it's really worth using your best olive oil to pour over at the end.

Heat the oil in a saucepan over a low heat. Add the garlic and fry briefly until it just begins to colour. Add the courgettes and a good pinch of salt and some pepper. Cook for 5–10 minutes, stirring occasionally, so they begin to soften and colour slightly. Add 3 tablespoons of the water (or chicken stock), cover and continue cooking for a further 10 minutes or so. Make sure you stir the courgettes from time to time, you want them to be very soft.

Remove the lid, add the rest of the water, or chicken stock, and the beans. Season well at this stage. Cover and simmer for about 5 minutes, to allow the flavours to mix together. Turn off the heat and stir in the basil. Either serve hot or leave the soup to cool at room temperature before serving with the extra virgin olive oil poured over.

PAPPA *al* POMODORO – TOMATO, BREAD *and* BASIL SOUP

Serves 4

1kg ripe tomatoes

2 tbsp olive oil

2 garlic cloves, finely sliced

200ml water

150g stale strong white bread, crust removed and torn into pieces (sourdough or ciabatta work best)

40g basil, leaves picked and torn into pieces

2 tbsp extra virgin olive oil, plus extra for serving

salt and freshly ground black pepper

A wonderfully thick Tuscan soup using sweet, ripe tomatoes and fragrant basil. There are so few ingredients, it's worth using the best ones you can find. Try to make it at the height of summer when tomatoes are at their tastiest.

Make a small slit in the skin of each tomato and put them in a large bowl. Pour over boiling water to cover. Leave for at least 30 seconds, then drain and run under cold water until cool enough to handle. Peel off the skins, which should come away easily. Keep the peeled tomatoes in the bowl to catch the juice and using your hands or the tip of a knife, dig out the white core and most of the seedy centre, reserving it in a separate bowl.

Place a saucepan over a medium heat and add the oil. Add the garlic and cook until it is just starting to colour. This will take less than a minute, so keep an eye on it.

Add the skinned tomato pieces and their juices to the pan. Add a good pinch of salt and stir well.

Strain any remaining juice from the seeds and skin left in the other bowl, into the pan and discard the seeds and skin.

Cook the tomatoes over a medium heat for 10–15 minutes or until they start to break apart and blend together. Lay the pieces of bread on top of the tomatoes and pour in just enough water to soak the bread. Turn off the heat and leave to cool for at least 15 minutes.

To finish, sprinkle over the basil and drizzle with the extra virgin olive oil. Gently fold the bread and herbs into the tomatoes and season well.

Serve at room temperature in shallow bowls with a good glug of olive oil poured over the top.

GLOBE ARTICHOKES
with VINAIGRETTE

Serves 2

2 globe artichokes

salt

For the vinaigrette

1 garlic clove, crushed to a
paste with salt

2 tsp Dijon mustard

3 tsp red wine vinegar

6 tbsp extra virgin olive oil

salt and freshly ground
black pepper

The best and simplest introduction for those who haven't cooked fresh artichokes before. No cutting or paring is needed and all the work is done by the eater. Artichokes are easy to take with you on a picnic and are great fun for children too. The prize is reaching the sweet heart at the end.

Find a large pot big enough to accommodate both artichokes. Fill it with salted water and bring to the boil. Add the artichokes and cook for 25 minutes, or until a skewer or knife inserted into the thickest part, just above the stem, meets no resistance. Remove from the water and set aside to cool.

While the artichokes are cooking, prepare the vinaigrette. If you've used a pestle and mortar to crush the garlic, you could make the vinaigrette in this. Otherwise, put the crushed garlic into a bowl with the mustard. Whisk in the vinegar and then the oil, drop by drop at first, then in a steady, very thin stream whisking all the while. As the oil is incorporated, the mixture will thicken. When all the oil is whisked in, season well with salt and pepper.

To serve, give each person an artichoke. Peel off the petals, one by one, and dip the thick, pulpy end of the petal into the vinaigrette. Once you reach the choke, cut out the hairy centre and eat the smooth, fleshy heart.

POTATO, CORNICHON *and* MUSTARD SALAD

Serves 2

500g new potatoes

1 tbsp thinly sliced shallot

1 large tsp Dijon mustard

2 tsp red wine vinegar

1 tbsp extra virgin olive oil

4 or 5 cornichons, chopped

1 tsp small capers or 2 tsp large capers, chopped

2 handfuls of mixed salad leaves (watercress, rocket, lambs lettuce, sorrel, mustard leaf)

salt and freshly ground black pepper

Good, fresh ingredients are the key to making a beautiful salad. New potatoes have a lovely waxy texture and sweet taste, and this is an excellent chance to use a variety of salad leaves if you can get your hands on them or — even better — have grown them yourself.

Bring a pan of water to the boil. Add 1 teaspoon of salt and the potatoes and boil for 15–20 minutes, or until the potatoes are tender when you insert a fork. Drain and transfer to a bowl to set aside and cool completely.

Put the sliced shallot in the pan with the mustard and vinegar along with a good pinch of salt.

When the potatoes are cool enough to handle, halve them or cut them into bite-sized pieces. Add them to the macerating shallots with the olive oil. Add the cornichons and capers and some salt and pepper and mix well.

To serve, throw in the salad leaves and toss everything together well.

BARLEY, SALTED RICOTTA *and* TOMATO SALAD

Serves 2

100g pearl barley

200g cherry
tomatoes, halved

½ red onion, finely sliced

zest of ½ lemon

2 tsp lemon juice

2 tbsp extra virgin olive oil

200g salted ricotta or
feta, sliced

1 tbsp chopped oregano
or marjoram

salt and freshly ground
black pepper

This is a simple but incredibly tasty and filling salad. Salted ricotta has a firm texture and holds its shape when sliced, but feta also works very well. The pearl barley adds a lovely nuttiness, while the tomato and herbs provide a burst of freshness.

Bring a large saucepan of salted water to the boil. Pour in the pearl barley and simmer, covered, for 10–12 minutes, or until tender. Drain and rinse well under cold water.

Shake the barley dry and return it to the pan along with the tomatoes, onion, lemon zest and juice and oil. Season with salt and pepper and mix well.

Finally, gently fold in the ricotta and herbs.

QUINOA SALAD
with AVOCADO, CUCUMBER *and* CHILLI

Serves 2

100g quinoa, well rinsed

1 garlic clove, crushed to a paste with salt

1 tsp sherry vinegar

1 tsp red wine vinegar

2 tbsp olive oil

1 ripe avocado, deseeded and cubed

1 red chilli, deseeded and finely chopped

1 cucumber, peeled, deseeded and cubed

2 spring onions, finely sliced

150g radishes, thinly sliced

2 tbsp each of chopped mint, parsley and coriander

salt and freshly ground black pepper

A wonderful good-for-you dish that's bright with herbs and has an added kick of chilli. Perfect as a lunchtime salad, eaten at home or taken as a packed lunch.

Bring a large pan of salted water to the boil. Add the quinoa and simmer for 10–12 minutes, or until just tender. Refresh under cold water, then drain well again and return to the cooled pan.

Add the garlic and vinegars to the quinoa and give it a good mix through. Stir in the olive oil and season with salt and pepper.

Add all the other ingredients to the pan and gently mix together before serving.

SPANISH BUTTER BEAN *and* TUNA SALAD

Serves 2

1 garlic clove, crushed to a paste with salt

2 tbsp sherry vinegar

4 tbsp extra virgin olive oil

½ red onion, finely sliced

1 tin (400g) butter beans, rinsed

250g cherry tomatoes, halved

50g pitted black olives

20g flat-leaf parsley, roughly chopped

1 tin (200g) sustainably sourced tuna, drained

salt and freshly ground black pepper

This full-flavoured salad is one of my favourite easy-to-make lunches. Apart from the tomatoes and parsley, all of the ingredients can be found in the store cupboard, so it's a great dish to throw together at the last minute and take with you as a packed lunch.

In a large bowl, whisk together the garlic, vinegar and olive oil. Season with salt and pepper.

Add the onion, butter beans, tomatoes, olives and parsley and mix well.

Gently stir in the tuna, being careful not to break it up too much.

SOBA NOODLE SALAD

Serves 1–2

160g soba noodles

1 tbsp groundnut or
light olive oil

2 tbsp sesame seeds

2 tsp caster sugar

1 tbsp soy sauce

2 tbsp water

2 tbsp rice wine vinegar

2cm piece ginger,
finely grated

1 red chilli, deseeded and
finely chopped

20g coriander, chopped

1 cucumber, peeled,
deseeded and sliced

4 spring onions,
finely chopped

In Japan, soba noodles are traditionally served in a flavoursome, steaming hot broth. These noodles are extremely good at soaking up flavour, but in this salad the noodles impart their own delicious, nutty taste. Instead of using cucumber you could use edamame beans, or serve the salad with a piece of grilled fish for something more filling.

Cook the soba noodles in plenty of salted, boiling water for about 3 minutes. After this time they should still be a little firm.

Drain and rinse thoroughly under cold water. Once drained, toss the noodles with the oil to prevent them from sticking. Set aside.

Make the dressing. Pound together the sesame seeds with the sugar in a large pestle and mortar, then add the soy sauce and water and mix to form a light paste. Stir in the rice wine vinegar and mix well. Taste and adjust as necessary.

Add the noodles to the dressing, lifting the strands up to coat well. Add the ginger, chilli, coriander, cucumber and spring onion and toss together well.

WARM SALAD *of* CHARD *and* CHICKPEAS

Serves 4

300g chard, leaves tough
stalks removed

1 tbsp olive oil

2 medium carrots,
peeled and cubed

4 celery stalks, cut into
2cm slices

2 garlic cloves, sliced

1 tsp dried chilli flakes

1 tin (400g) cooked
chickpeas, drained
and rinsed

2 tbsp tahini paste

juice of 1 lemon

1 tbsp extra virgin olive oil

90ml water

1 tbsp chopped
flat-leaf parsley

salt and freshly ground
black pepper

This is an ideal vegetarian main or side dish. The recipe calls for tahini, a sesame seed paste that is used a lot in Middle Eastern cooking, and it makes a wonderful creamy sauce for this salad. Although this dish is lovely warm, it can also be eaten at room temperature and is delicious the following day as the flavours continue to develop overnight.

Bring a large pan of salted water to the boil. Add the chard stalks and blanch for 2 minutes. Then add the leaves and cook for a further 1 minute. Drain and roughly chop, then set aside.

Return the pan to a low heat and add the oil. Add the carrots and celery with a good pinch of salt and gently fry for about 5 minutes so they begin to soften and colour slightly. Add the garlic and chilli flakes and cook for a further couple of minutes.

Stir in the chickpeas and season well with salt and pepper. Cook for a further 1–2 minutes to allow the flavours to combine. Take off the heat and set aside.

In a large bowl, mix the tahini, lemon juice, olive oil and water until you have a smooth sauce. Add the tahini sauce to the chickpea mixture along with the chopped chard and the parsley. Stir together gently to mix, and serve.

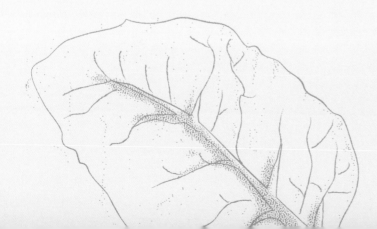

ITALIAN RAGOUT
of VEGETABLES

Serves 4

4 tbsp olive oil

1 red onion,
finely sliced

1 head garlic, cloves
peeled and left whole

500g red peppers,
deseeded and thinly sliced

500g waxy potatoes, peeled
and cut into 2cm cubes

500g aubergines, cut into
2cm cubes

300g tomatoes, white
core removed and roughly
chopped

15g bunch of marjoram or
oregano, roughly chopped

2 tbsp red wine vinegar

salt and freshly ground
black pepper

extra virgin olive oil,
for serving

Vegetables cooked together slowly develop a wonderful flavour that simply improves over time. The potatoes make this a complete meal in itself but it also works well as an antipasto or served as a side dish with roast meat.

Place a large, heavy-based pan with a lid over a low heat. Add 2 tablespoons of oil, the onion and a pinch of salt. Gently sweat the onion for about 10 minutes or until it begins to soften. Add the garlic cloves and peppers and continue to cook, stirring occasionally for a further 10–15 minutes. When the mixture is soft and almost stew-like, transfer to a plate.

Add the remaining oil to the empty pan, return to high heat. When it is hot, put in the potatoes along with a pinch of salt and cook for a few minutes, stirring frequently so they don't stick. Add the aubergines and continue to cook for a further 5 minutes, or until the vegetables begin to soften. Add the tomatoes and cook for 10–15 minutes or until they collapse and form a sauce. Season well with salt and pepper. Return the onion and pepper mixture to the pan with the chopped marjoram and vinegar and stir everything together well. Reduce the heat to low, partially cover the pan with a lid and cook for 15–20 minutes, stirring occasionally so the mixture doesn't stick. The aubergines and tomatoes should turn into a thick, unctuous sauce and coat the other vegetables, which will become perfectly tender while still retaining some shape.

Serve at room temperature with extra virgin olive oil poured on top and some good bread.

PARTY POTS

Dishes to celebrate with

Cooking for friends or a party of people is a lovely thing to do, but you want the atmosphere to feel as relaxed as possible. This is when cooking in one pot really comes into its own.

I like nothing better than putting a big plate of beautiful-looking food onto the table for everyone to help themselves. It creates a great sense of feasting and makes the party feel convivial and informal.

Dishes often look wonderful served in the pot or pan they've been cooked in — like chicken roasted on celeriac and potatoes or seafood paella scattered with mussels and clams. Some dishes, like the Moroccan New Year chicken with couscous look beautiful generously piled onto a great big plate or serving dish. Getting your guests involved and allowing them to help themselves makes your job easier and the party more fun.

All the recipes in this chapter serve four to six people, but the quantities can be easily increased or decreased. Keep in mind that, when you're cooking fish, allow 150-200g per person. For meat, allow 200–300g per person.

Most of the dishes don't need to be served with anything more than a salad or some bread, but if you're making a real feast, consider pairing a couple dishes. Whole roast turbot on potatoes and fennel is delicious served with the summer bean ragout. Or if you're really putting on a show, make one of the dishes as a starter (I love the black squid risotto) and follow it with another recipe for your main course. End the evening with a one-pot pudding and, before you know it, you'll be ready to have a party every week!

FISH CHOWDER

Serves 6

30g butter

250g smoked
bacon lardons

1 large onion, finely diced

2 medium carrots, diced

2 celery stalks, diced

500g potatoes, peeled
and cubed

2 corn on the cob, kernels
or 1 tin (400g) sweetcorn

300ml white wine

300ml single cream

a small bunch of thyme

1 bay leaf

250g haddock fillet

250g smoked
haddock fillet

300g clams

300g mussels

20g flat-leaf parsley,
chopped

salt and freshly ground
black pepper

Originating in North America, chowder is a wonderfully flavoursome stew that is a meal in itself. The smoked bacon and haddock adds a great depth. Use a fairly large pot because the shellfish take up quite a lot of room when they open. I like it served with a cold glass of real ale.

Prepare the shellfish. Thow away any shells that are open, broken or won't close if given a sharp tap against a bench top. Now wash them in cold water, removing the beard from the mussels (the fibrous clinging tuft of hair attached to the shell). Set aside.

Melt the butter in a large, heavy-based pan over a medium heat. Fry the lardons so they become brown and crisp. Then add the onions, carrots and celery along with a good pinch of salt. Cook gently for 10–15 minutes, stirring occasionally so the mixture softens but be careful not to let it brown.

Add the potatoes and sweetcorn, then season and stir well. Pour over the wine and let it boil to evaporate by about half. Add the cream, thyme and bay leaf, then top up with water just to cover. Partially cover and cook for 20–25 minutes, or until the potatoes become soft.

Put the fish in first, followed by the shellfish. Cover and poach gently for 5–10 minutes or until the clams and mussels open and the fish is cooked.

Taste for seasoning and serve with chopped parsley on top.

BLACK RISOTTO
with SQUID

Serves 4–6

2 tbsp olive oil

1 red onion, finely diced

3 garlic cloves, finely chopped

1 tsp thyme leaves

½ tsp dried chilli flakes

1 tsp fennel seeds, ground

450g squid including the tentacles, cleaned and cut into strips

300g risotto rice

100ml white wine

12g (about 4 sachets) cuttlefish ink

1 litre hot fish stock, or water

a small knob of unsalted butter

2 tbsp chopped flat-leaf parsley

salt and freshly ground black pepper

A spectacular-looking dish to serve to friends. The black ink from cuttlefish gives this dish its wonderful colour; you can buy it in sachets either from the supermarket or a fishmonger. The risotto has a deep and unusual flavour, but the method is the same for any risotto.

In a large, heavy-bottomed pan, heat the oil over a medium heat. Add the onion along with a pinch of salt and gently fry until it begins to soften but not colour. Now add the garlic and continue to cook for 1–2 minutes, then add the thyme leaves, chilli flakes and fennel seeds. Finally add the squid pieces and fry briefly until they start to curl.

Pour in the rice and stir well, coating every grain so it looks shiny. Season with salt and pepper.

Now add the wine, stirring for a minute before adding the cuttlefish ink. Stir until every grain of rice is coated in black ink, then add the hot stock, a ladle at a time. Stir gently until all the liquid has been absorbed before adding the next.

Continue stirring and adding the stock a ladle at a time for 20-30 minutes, or until the rice is soft but still has a bit of bite and the liquid around the rice is creamy. Stir in the butter and chopped parsley. Check the seasoning before serving.

SUMMER BEAN RAGOUT *with* OLIVES *and* HERBS

Serves 4–6

400g runner beans, topped and tailed

400g green beans, topped and tailed

3 tbsp olive oil

I red onion, finely chopped

4 garlic cloves, finely sliced

2 tins (800g) tomatoes

I tsp sugar

I tin (400g) borlotti beans

I tin (400g) cannellini beans

20g pitted black olives

20g of one of the following herbs or a mixture: mint, basil, parsley, marjoram, chopped

extra virgin olive oil

salt and freshly ground black pepper

Try to use as many fresh green beans as you can get your hands on and vary them for different textures and shapes if you like. Sometimes I add tinned tuna or anchovies and hard-boiled eggs, transforming this into a kind of Niçoise salad.

Fill a large, heavy-based pot with water and add 2 teaspoons salt. Place over a high heat and bring to the boil. Add the fresh beans to the boiling water, all at once if they fit, otherwise do this in batches. Blanch for about 2 minutes – they should still have a bit of bite – then remove and refresh under cold water. Drain and set aside. When all the beans are cooked, empty the pot and dry it.

Return the pan to a medium heat and add the oil. Add the onion along with a little salt and gently fry until it is just starting to colour and become soft. This should take 10–15 minutes. Add the garlic and cook for a further 1–2 minutes, then put in the tomatoes and sugar. Season well and cook gently for 20 minutes, or until the tomatoes break down into a thick, sweet sauce.

Add the tinned beans, the olives and half of the herbs to the sauce and cook together for about 5 minutes, then add the fresh beans and about 50ml water. Stir well and simmer gently for about 10 minutes. To finish, sprinkle over the rest of the herbs and drizzle over a glug of really good olive oil.

MEDFOUN – MOROCCAN NEW YEAR CHICKEN *with* COUSCOUS

Serves 6

For the chicken

1.5kg chicken thighs and legs

3 medium onions, chopped

2 tsp ground ginger

1 tsp ground black pepper

2 cinnamon sticks

½ tsp saffron threads, crumbled

2 tsp ground turmeric

2 tsp salt

1 tbsp olive oil

50g butter

2 large carrots, peeled and sliced

1 litre water

2 tbsp mix of fresh coriander and parsley, chopped

For the couscous

500g instant couscous

75g sultanas, soaked in boiling water for 20 minutes

1 tsp ground cinnamon

1 tsp icing sugar

2 tbsp toasted flaked almonds

Here is a proper celebratory dish from Morocco, often served there at New Year. It looks stunning piled up into a tall cone shape and decorated with cinnamon, flaked almonds and icing sugar. Place it in the centre of the table allowing guests to delve in and discover juicy, spiced chicken inside.

In a large bowl, put in the chicken pieces, onions, spices, salt and oil and mix together well.

Place a large, heavy-based pot with a lid on a medium heat and melt half of the butter. Add the chicken mixture and cook for 5–10 minutes, or until the chicken is lightly browned on all sides.

Put in the carrots, then pour over the water and bring to a simmer. Partially cover with a lid and cook for 40 minutes to 1 hour, or until the chicken pieces are tender.

Follow the packet instructions to cook the couscous. Then drain and add all the sultanas, the remaining butter, and half of the cinnamon, sugar and almonds, reserving the rest for decorating. Toss everything together gently and cover to keep warm.

When the chicken is tender and cooked, remove it, along with the cinnamon sticks, from the sauce. Turn up the heat and boil the mixture to reduce the liquid to about 500ml. Taste and adjust the seasoning as necessary. At this point, you can remove the chicken from the bones if you prefer.

To serve, put one-third of the couscous on a serving plate and lay the chicken on top. Sprinkle over the coriander and parsley. Pour over the sauce and cover with the remaining couscous in a dome shape.

Sprinkle over the remaining icing sugar and cinnamon to decorate and finally the toasted almonds in strips leading up from the base to the peak (see the finished dish on page 162).

SEAFOOD PAELLA

Serves 6

6 tbsp olive oil

a selection of any of the
following, with a total
weight of 1.5kg:

prawns in their shell

clams, cleaned

mussels, cleaned

squid, thickly sliced

scallops

monkfish or halibut pieces,
skin removed and cubed

1 large onion, diced

1 green pepper, deseeded
and finely chopped

4 garlic cloves, finely
chopped

350g paella rice

150ml white wine
or dry sherry

a pinch of saffron

1 litre hot fish stock
or water

juice of 1 lemon

20g bunch of flat-leaf
parsley, chopped

salt and freshly ground
black pepper

This looks striking yet it couldn't be easier to make. Unlike risotto, a paella is cooked without stirring, which gives it a wonderful caramelised base, where the rice has browned and become sticky. It's not necessary to use a paella pan — a normal frying pan will do the trick — just make sure it's large enough to hold all of the fish.

Prepare the shellfish as per page 152.

In a large, flat-based paella pan or frying pan, heat 4 tablespoons of the oil. Quickly fry the squid, scallops and fish pieces (if using), to brown all over. Remove and set aside.

Heat the rest of the oil in the pan and add the onion and pepper along with a good pinch of salt. Gently cook for 10 minutes then add the garlic and continue to cook for a further 5 minutes or so. Pour in the rice and season well, then stir to coat in the vegetables and oil.

Pour in the wine or sherry and sprinkle over the saffron. Let it bubble for a couple of minutes, then add the stock (or water) and season well. Turn the heat down to medium-low so the mixture bubbles just slightly.

From this point on, resist the temptation to stir the rice. The key to making paella is to allow the rice to cook in the stock, undisturbed. Let the paella cook, uncovered, for about 10 minutes; the rice will begin to absorb the stock and will start to look sticky.

Return the browned fish to the pan, then add the mussels, clams and prawns (if using). With a wooden spoon, gently dig them into the rice base. If it looks dry, add a splash more water, then cover with foil and cook for a further 10 minutes, so the mussels open and the fish cooks.

Turn off the heat and leave to sit for 5 minutes or so. Remove the foil; the rice should be sticky, cooked and brown at the edges.

Sprinkle over the lemon juice and parsley to serve.

WHOLE TURBOT ROASTED *over* POTATOES *and* FENNEL

Serves 6

1 whole turbot or brill weighing about 2kg, gutted, gills removed

20g flat-leaf parsley or fennel herb

4 tbsp olive oil

500g waxy potatoes, peeled and sliced

2 fennel bulbs, sliced

400g tomatoes, sliced

4 anchovy fillets, finely chopped

3 garlic cloves, crushed to a paste with salt

20g rosemary leaves, roughly chopped

salt and freshly ground black pepper

Roasting a whole fish keeps it succulent but also looks impressive served at the table. Turbot is a big, beautiful flatfish with firm white flesh. If you can't get hold of one, try using brill, which is equally delicious. Get your fishmonger to gut and clean the fish for you.

Heat the oven to 220°C/425°F/Gas 7.

Season the fish well and put the parsley or fennel herb into the cavity near its head and set aside.

Pour 3 tablespoons of olive oil into a deep baking dish large enough to hold the fish. Then add all the ingredients, except the fish, and mix really well so that the garlic, oil and anchovies coat the vegetables and everything is evenly distributed. Spread gently to form an even surface.

Roast, uncovered in the oven for 25–30 minutes, or until the vegetables are beginning to colour and soften. Remove and stir gently to break up the tomatoes and to give everything a chance to cook evenly. Now lay the fish on top of the vegetables. Pour over the remaining olive oil and return to the oven for a further 25 minutes.

To test if the fish is cooked, gently push a skewer through the thickest part. If there is no resistance, it is cooked through. Otherwise, return it to the oven for a little longer.

I usually present this as a whole fish lying on top of the juicy, roasted vegetables for people to portion up in the pan and help themselves.

FISH PIE

Serves 6

a selection of any of the following fish, skinned and cut into 2cm pieces, with a total weight of 1kg:

smoked haddock

salmon

pollock or sustainably caught cod

prawns, shelled and deveined

1 bay leaf

8 black peppercorns

400ml full-fat milk

50g butter

2 level tbsp plain flour, plus extra for rolling

50ml white wine (optional)

3 tsp capers, rinsed

80g Cheddar cheese, grated

200g spinach, roughly chopped

20g flat-leaf parsley, roughly chopped

300g puff pastry

salt and freshly ground black pepper

1 egg, lightly beaten, for glazing

The puff pastry topping makes a light alternative to the usual mashed potato so you can afford more richness in the filling. You can vary the fish or use a different combination according to what's available and fresh. The whole pie could be prepared in advance, then baked when you're ready to eat.

Heat the oven to 180°C/350°F/Gas 4.

In a low-sided, large casserole, add the fish pieces along with the bay leaf, peppercorns and milk and bring to a simmer, by which time the fish will be almost cooked. Transfer the fish to a plate and strain the milk into a jug.

Give the pan a wash and return to the heat. Melt the butter until it is bubbling and then add the flour. Stir together and cook until it begins to brown lightly. Pour over the milk and whisk well to make a smooth sauce. Continue to cook on a low heat to allow the sauce to thicken until it coats the back of a spoon. Season well with salt and pepper and add the wine (if using). Cook, stirring for another few minutes and allow it to thicken a little more.

Add the capers, cheese, spinach and parsley to the pan and mix well. Return the fish to the pan and gently fold all the ingredients together.

On a lightly floured surface, roll out the pastry to 5mm thick and place it over the top of the casserole to form a lid. Trim off any excess pastry and discard. Brush over some beaten egg and bake in the oven for 30–40 minutes or until the top is brown and crisp.

KERALAN FISH CURRY

Serves 4–6

For the fish

about 900g kingfish fillets
(or other white meaty fish)

juice of 2 limes

2 tsp ground turmeric

½ tsp cayenne pepper

For the curry

½ tsp fenugreek seeds

1 tbsp coconut oil,
or light olive oil

2 tsp mustard seeds

1 red onion,
finely chopped

3 garlic cloves,
finely chopped

1cm piece ginger, peeled
and finely chopped

2–3 green chillies,
deseeded and finely
chopped

2 tsp coriander seeds

200g chopped tin
tomatoes

1 green mango, peeled,
deseeded and cut into
small pieces

400g runner beans or okra

2 tbsp tamarind paste

1 tin (250ml) coconut milk

For this recipe, get everything chopped up and ready beforehand, then just enjoy standing over the pot, stirring things in and smelling the scent of the spices as the curry develops. Unripe mangoes hold their shape well and add a good tartness to the curry, and they work well with the tamarind. If you can't find them just use potatoes or squash to get a similar texture.

Cut the fish into roughly 3cm pieces and marinate in a bowl with the lime juice, turmeric, chilli powder and some salt. Set aside.

In a large pan, toast the fenugreek and coriander seeds over a medium heat for 1–2 minutes or until they crackle and release their fragrance. Grind them in a pestle and mortar and set aside. In the same pan, heat the oil and gently fry the mustard seeds until they start to crackle and pop. Add the ground coriander, fenugreek and the onion and cook gently for 5 minutes or so, until it starts to soften. Add some salt along with the garlic, ginger and chillies and cook together for 10 minutes.

Now stir in the tomatoes and season well. Cook for another 5 minutes or so, then add the mango, beans or okra, tamarind paste and enough water to almost cover. Stir well and cook everything together until the beans begin to soften. Finally, add the coconut milk and cook for a few minutes, tasting for seasoning.

Gently stir in the fish and let it cook in the rich sauce until it is just done (depending on the size of the pieces, this should take between 3–6 minutes). Turn off the heat and let it sit for a couple of minutes to absorb the rest of the flavours.

This curry is delicious served with a few naan breads or some steaming hot rice.

CHICKEN BIRYANI

Serves 6

500g basmati rice

50g unsalted butter

1 tbsp olive oil

2 medium onions, sliced

1.5cm piece ginger, peeled and finely chopped

2 tsp cumin seeds

2 tsp coriander seeds

2 tsp ground turmeric

8 cardamom pods

½ cinnamon stick

6 chicken thighs

2 tbsp yoghurt, plus extra to serve

30g flaked almonds

20g coriander leaves, chopped

salt and freshly ground black pepper

A very fragrant Indian dish of spicy rice steamed over braised chicken. Cooked in this way the rice becomes fluffy and light while the chicken remains juicy and succulent underneath. It needs very little in the way of accompaniment, maybe some cucumber raita or chutney on the table.

Wash the rice and soak it in plenty of warm water along with a teaspoon of salt.

In a heavy-based pan with a lid, melt the butter and oil over a medium heat. Add the onion with a good pinch of salt and fry gently, for 10 minutes or so, until it is very soft and translucent. Add the ginger and the spices and cook for a little longer, then add the chicken pieces and season well. Fry for a few minutes, to lightly brown the chicken on all sides. Finally, stir in the yoghurt and the almonds and mix well.

Cut a piece of baking parchment into a circle slightly larger than the size of the pan lid. Place it on top of the chicken and cover with the lid and cook for about 15 minutes on a low heat, or until tender. Remove the baking parchment and lid.

Drain the rice and pour it over the chicken. Add cold water to just 1cm above the surface of the rice, then cover again with the baking parchment and the lid and bring to the boil. Turn the heat down to low and simmer for 15 minutes, then turn off the heat and allow the rice to sit with the lid on for a further 10 minutes.

To serve, sprinkle the coriander on top and add a dollop of yoghurt.

CHICKEN ROASTED OVER CELERIAC *and* POTATOES

Serves 4-6

1 chicken, weighing 2kg

800g potatoes, peeled and sliced into 1cm pieces

800g celeriac, peeled and sliced into 1cm pieces

3 garlic cloves, very finely chopped

1 tbsp olive oil

20g thyme, leaves picked

200ml single cream

50g butter, cut into 2 pieces

100ml white wine

salt and freshly ground black pepper

This dish looks beautiful as it emerges from the oven — a golden roast bird sitting on layers of creamy celeriac and potatoes. All the juices from the chicken seep into the vegetables as it cooks. A fresh green salad and someone to carve is all you need for a feast.

Heat the oven to 170°C/350°F/Gas 3½.

Add the sliced potatoes and celeriac along with the garlic, oil and half of the thyme and cream to a large baking tray. Season well and mix together. Arrange the slices so they lie more or less flat to provide an even base for the chicken to rest on.

Slide your fingers under the skin of each chicken breast and tuck a piece of butter and the rest of the thyme in each.

Season the chicken well, inside and out, and rest it on the potatoes, breast-side down.

Pour over the wine and put in the oven to roast for 50 minutes.

After this time, take it out and turn the chicken over so its breast faces up and continue to cook for a further 30 minutes. Remove from the oven and check it is cooked through by inserting a skewer into the flesh just above the leg. Once inserted, the juices should run clear.

Cover loosely with foil and leave to rest for up to 30 minutes.

To serve, carve the chicken or cut into joints and serve with the roasted potatoes and celeriac.

POT-AU-FEU

Serves 6–8

1kg brisket or silverside, rolled and tied

600g ox cheek (optional)

700g oxtail

700g leeks

700g carrots

300g parsnips

300g turnips

200g celery

200g large tomatoes

parsley and thyme stalks and a bay leaf tied into a bundle

salt and freshly ground black pepper

To serve

Dijon mustard

creamed horseradish

cornichons

A typical French dish in which the most is made of inexpensive cuts of meat, slow cooked to melting tenderness in a vegetable broth. It's worth putting all the raw ingredients into the pot first to check they will all fit. Weights of meat are approximate, a little more or less is up to the cook.

Put all the meat pieces into a large, deep ovenproof pot. Cover with cold water and bring to the boil. You will find that lots of foamy scum rises to the surface. Skim it off with a large spoon and you will have a much clearer, cleaner-tasting broth. When you have removed all the scum, add more cold water to replace the liquid you have skimmed off.

Turn the heat down to a simmer. Continue to skim any scum that comes to the surface until the bubbles start to look clean (this will take about 15 minutes), topping up with cold water as necessary. Adding the cold water not only keeps sufficient liquid in the pot, but also helps to bring all the scum to the surface.

Add 1 teaspoon of salt at this point.

During the skimming process, prepare the vegetables. Trim the leeks, remove their outer layers and cut them into thirds. Peel the carrots and keep them whole, peel the parsnips and turnips and cut them, along with the celery and tomatoes into large pieces. The larger the pieces the better, as they will hold their shape while cooking.

Add the vegetables and herb bundle to the pot with 1 teaspoon of salt and a few grindings of pepper. If necessary, lift the meat to ensure the vegetables are well submerged in the broth.

Partially cover, to allow some steam to escape, and simmer for 3 hours. Keep an eye on it and skim off any more scum that may appear, topping up with cold water as necessary.

Remove the meat and the vegetables from the broth. Discard the tomatoes, turnips and parsnip – these have played their part by imparting all their flavour.

Taste the broth and adjust the seasoning. There will be some fat on the surface. You can scoop it off with a spoon, or lay a piece of kitchen paper on to it to absorb it.

Slice the cooked meat and serve with the leeks, carrots and ladle a spoonful of broth over each serving.

Put the mustard, horseradish and cornichons on the table for everyone to help themselves.

GUINEA FOWL, CABBAGE *and* CHESTNUT PIE

Serves 6

2 tbsp olive oil

1 guinea fowl, weighing about 1.5kg, jointed into 6 pieces

3 medium onions, finely chopped

4 garlic cloves, finely sliced

3 or 4 celery stalks

150g smoked, streaky bacon, chopped

20g mixed bunch of rosemary, sage and thyme leaves, chopped

200g peeled and cooked chestnuts

200ml red wine

500ml chicken stock

2 bay leaves

½ tsp juniper berries

400g cabbage, shredded

100g puff pastry

plain flour, for dusting

1 egg, lightly beaten, for glazing

salt and freshly ground black pepper

Guinea fowl has a richer flavour than chicken and tastes delicious with sweet chestnuts. You can, of course, use chicken or even a game bird like pheasant as an alternative. A large, low-sided casserole dish is perfect for this. With the pastry baked on top, you can serve it straight out of the pot.

Preheat the oven to 160°C/325°F/Gas 3.

Place a large, low-sided casserole over a medium heat and add the oil. Add the guinea fowl pieces and brown on all sides. Remove to a plate. Lower the heat under the pan and add the onions, garlic, celery and bacon with a good pinch of salt. Gently sweat until soft and sweet – this should take at least 10–15 minutes. Add the chopped herbs and chestnuts and cook a little more, then add the wine. Bring to the boil to burn off some of the alcohol, then add the stock, bay leaves and juniper berries. Tuck the guinea fowl pieces into the casserole and cover with a lid.

Simmer for 45 minutes–1 hour, or until the meat is cooked through but still juicy and falls off the bone easily.

Remove the meat from the casserole and shred, then return to the pan, discarding any bones. Add the shredded cabbage and stir everything into the cooking juices. Taste and adjust the seasoning. Put the lid back on and return to the heat for a few minutes to finish cooking the cabbage.

Roll out the pastry to a sheet slightly larger than the casserole lid and about 5mm thick. (A thin layer of pastry on top makes a delicious pie.) Lay the pastry over the surface of the pie mixture and up the sides, tucking it under around the edge to make a neat lid. Brush over some beaten egg and place in the oven to bake for 30 minutes, or until the top is golden and crisp.

Remove from the oven and serve immediately.

SWEET POTS

Puddings, cakes and delicious desserts

Treating yourself or your guests to pudding doesn't require complicated kit or laborious techniques. These sweet pots are so simple and fun to make, and of course, utterly delicious.

In the recipes that follow, I've taken a rather loose approach to 'one pot' but the recipes are so uncomplicated that you really won't notice the addition of a couple of other simple bits of kit that are essential to make a decent pudding.

The techniques for these sweet pots are neither hard nor time-consuming. When it comes to whisking eggs, you don't need to have an electric mixer. It is quicker if you do, but all of these recipes can be made by hand — the old-fashioned way.

These sweet pots are ideal for cooks in a rush as you can easily make them ahead of time. In the case of the tiramisu, making it a day in advance simply improves everything about it, and allows the sponge fingers to soften as they soak up all the flavour.

In this chapter, there are easy desserts that can be made throughout the year: in summer, try the rhubarb and stem ginger fool or strawberries with frozen lemon. Autumn is the best time for blackberries, so try the blackberry clafoutis or roast figs with mascarpone. In winter, when you're after some comfort from the cold outside, steamed lemon pudding or little chocolate and orange pots will give you some warmth. And when you crave something a little less rich and indulgent, I've included healthy and light options too, like poached summer fruit salad with peaches and apricots or the refreshing watermelon granita.

These sweet pots will delight at any party and, if made in advance, they are extremely fuss-free. Then again, you don't need the excuse of a party just to enjoy a bit of an indulgence now and then.

POACHED SUMMER
FRUIT SALAD

Serves 4

3 peaches, stoned
and halved

4 apricots, stoned
and halved

1 star anise

1 bay leaf

½ vanilla pod, split and
seeds scraped

peel of ½ orange

juice of 1 orange

100ml white wine

2 tbsp honey

200g raspberries
(optional)

A delicate and light dessert which is perfect after a hearty meal. It can be prepared in advance then warmed, or eaten cool. The vibrant colours of the cooked summer fruit are stunning. To serve, try sprinkling over rose petals — they look beautiful and taste delicious. Any leftovers can be eaten for breakfast with crunchy granola and a dollop of yoghurt. Play around with the fruit you use and alter it according to the seasons.

In a medium-sized saucepan with a lid, add the peaches and apricots along with the rest of the ingredients apart from the raspberries. Set on a low heat, cover and simmer for 10 minutes to allow the fruit to release its juices. A couple of minutes before the end of cooking, add the raspberries, if using.

With a slotted spoon, remove the fruit from the liquid and place into serving bowls. If you prefer a thicker syrup, you can boil the liquid for a few more minutes to reduce it. Strain the syrup over the fruit through a sieve and serve with cream or crème fraîche.

STRAWBERRY *and* LEMONGRASS JELLY

Makes 4 jellies, each measuring 170ml

800g strawberries, hulled and quartered

250g caster sugar

juice of 1 lemon

2 lemongrass stalks, finely sliced

7 leaves gelatine (also check packet instructions)

The subtle fragrance of lemongrass makes this simple strawberry jelly taste even better. As an alternative, you could try adding crushed mint leaves to the heated strawberries.

Place a pan over a medium heat and add the strawberries (reserving a few to decorate the jelly with at the end) along with the sugar, lemon juice and lemongrass. Bring the mixture to the boil then simmer gently for a minute to allow the strawberries to soften. Remove from the heat and leave it to sit for a few minutes to infuse.

Strain the strawberry mixture through a sieve into a measuring jug, pushing as much of the pulp through as you can. If this creates a lot of foam on top, scooping it off with a spoon will give you a clearer jelly.

Measure the quantity of liquid (it should be around 700ml) and soak as many gelatine leaves as required for the amount of liquid (refer to the directions on the packet, although I find it's usually 1 leaf for every 100ml). Put the leaves in a bowl and cover with cold water for 5 minutes until they become soft and wobbly.

Squeeze the liquid out of the leaves and add them to the strawberry mixture. Put the strawberry mixture back into the pan and heat very gently, stirring the liquid to dissolve the gelatine.

Pour the mixture into a jelly mould or individual glasses and allow to cool. Refrigerate for at least 3 hours to set. If you want a firmer set to the jelly, you could leave them in the fridge overnight. Just before serving, decorate with the remaining strawberries.

BANANA *and* RUM
TARTE TATIN

Serves 4–6

3 bananas

50g unsalted butter

100g caster sugar

1 tbsp rum

1 tsp ground cinnamon

fresh nutmeg

zest of 1 orange

plain flour, for dusting

150g puff pastry

crème fraîche, for serving

This looks very elegant, and the combination of banana, rum and sticky caramel is heavenly. You can try different ways to slice and arrange the bananas to create any pattern you like. The trick with tarte tatin is to roll the puff pastry until it is really fine. That way the pastry will be perfectly crisp.

Heat the oven to 180°C/350°F/Gas 4.

Peel the bananas and cut them in half and then slice lengthways into thin strips.

To make the caramel, place a deep ovenproof frying pan or tarte pan over a medium heat and add the butter. When it is bubbling, add the sugar and let it melt without stirring. Cook until the mixture begins to caramelise and turn golden brown. Remove from the heat immediately.

Pour the rum into the caramel along with the cinnamon and a couple gratings of nutmeg. If it begins to separate, give it a good whisk. Put the caramel back on the stove over a low heat and cook for a minute, then arrange the bananas on top, taking care not to burn your fingers on the hot caramel.

Grate the orange zest over the bananas. Take off the heat and set aside.

On a floured surface, roll out the pastry to 3mm in thickness and roughly the size of the pan. It's important that it is quite thin. Drape the pastry over the rolling pin and carefully lift it to lay it over the bananas in the pan. Tuck the pastry in at the edges. Bake for 30–35 minutes, or until risen and golden in colour.

Remove from the oven. Place a serving plate, slightly larger than the pan, upside down on top of the pan. Wearing oven gloves, hold the plate and pan tightly together, then quickly invert the tarte onto the plate. Serve hot with crème fraîche.

RHUBARB FOOL
with STEM GINGER

Serves 4

400g rhubarb, trimmed
and cut into 1cm pieces

70g stem ginger, chopped
up into small pieces

50g caster sugar

juice of ½ lemon

300ml whipping cream

Rhubarb and ginger are made for each other. This looks very pretty served in glasses so you can see the colourful rippled-pink effect. Be careful not to over-whip the cream. It is better to under-whip it and then just stir it with the whisk until it reaches the perfect consistency.

Place a heavy-based saucepan with a lid over a low heat. Add the rhubarb, stem ginger, sugar and lemon juice. Heat very slowly and cook, covered for 5–10 minutes, or until the sugar melts and the rhubarb softens and begins to break apart.

The rhubarb will release some liquid but if it looks like there is a lot of liquid left when the rhubarb is all done, take off the lid, turn up the heat, and boil to reduce. You should have a thick purée. Take off the heat and allow to cool.

Whisk the cream until soft peaks form, then gently fold the cooled rhubarb purée through it, leaving broad streaks. Spoon into individual glasses or serve in the bowl you used for mixing.

DATE *and* ORANGE CAKE

150g unsalted butter, plus
extra for greasing

100g light brown sugar

2 eggs

200g self-raising flour

1 tsp ground cinnamon

75g ground almonds

a pinch of salt

2-3 large oranges – the zest
of one and a total of
175ml juice

200g chopped dates

30g candied peel, plus
extra for decorating

50g icing sugar

Lightly spiced, moist and naturally sweet with dates, this cake makes a wonderful pudding served warm with just a dollop of yoghurt or crème fraîche. Any leftovers can be eaten up at tea time.

Preheat the oven to 180°C/350°F/Gas 4.

Butter a 1 lb loaf tin and line with baking parchment. Add the butter and sugar to a bowl and beat together until light and fluffy. Mix in the eggs one by one, adding 1 tablespoon flour after each. Gently fold in the remaining flour, cinnamon, almonds and the salt. Add the orange zest, then loosen the mixture with 100ml of the orange juice to make a smooth batter. Fold in the chopped dates and candied peel and spoon the mixture into the lined loaf tin.

Bake for 1–1½ hours, or until a skewer inserted into the middle of the cake comes out clean.

Remove from the oven and use a skewer to pierce holes in the top of the cake. Leave to cool on a wire rack for 5 minutes before turning out and peeling away the baking parchment. Mix the remaining 75ml of orange juice with the icing sugar to make a smooth glaze. Pour this over the cake then sprinkle over the reserved candied peel.

WATERMELON GRANITA

Serves 6

1kg watermelon, skin removed and cut into large pieces

150g caster sugar

juice of 2 limes

a pinch of salt

Deliciously fresh-tasting and fantastically straightforward to make, granita is especially good for those times when you want something palate-cleansing and not too heavy. Serve spoonfuls of these sparkling, fruity pink crystals in chilled glasses.

Remove as many of the seeds as possible from the watermelon pieces. Add the watermelon pieces to a blender along with the sugar, lime juice and a pinch of salt. Push the mixture through a sieve into a shallow container, discard any leftover seeds and put the mixture into the freezer. After about 1 hour, remove from the freezer and whisk the mixture well, taking care to really scrape around the sides where the mixture can stick.

Put it back in the freezer. After about 1 hour, give it another good stir. Return it to the freezer until it is completely frozen yet still forkable. Now take a strong fork to the surface and chip it into a mass of crystals. Pile the frosted scrapings into already chilled small glasses and serve.

If you want to make this in advance, just cover it with a piece of baking parchment and store in the freezer where it will keep for up to 2 days until you're ready to serve.

STRAWBERRIES *with* FROZEN WHIPPED LEMON CREAM

Serves 4

200ml whipping cream

2 tbsp icing sugar

zest of 1 lemon

juice of 1½ lemons

400g strawberries, hulled and quartered

This is a wonderfully cooling and summery frozen pudding that can be made a day in advance. Serve it in individual glasses, or if you like, tea cups. The recipe works well with peaches too.

Whisk together the cream, 1 tablespoon icing sugar, half of the lemon zest and the juice of 1 lemon. It will quickly begin to thicken.

Scoop a generous spoonful of the lemon cream into each glass and freeze for at least 1 hour.

Meanwhile, put the strawberries in a bowl. Stir in the remaining lemon zest and juice along with the remaining tablespoon of icing sugar.

Remove the frozen whipped cream from the freezer and serve it with the strawberries on top. Pour any remaining juice over each glass too.

BAKED PEARS
WITH SPICES *and*
CHOCOLATE

Serves 6

6 pears, peeled

100ml marsala

4 tbsp soft brown sugar

I tsp ground cinnamon

½ vanilla pod

70g good-quality dark
chocolate

crème fraîche, to serve
(optional)

An elegant yet simple pudding, lightly spiced baked pears with melted chocolate is a classic combination not to mention a great way to use English pears in season. The chocolate is gently grated over at the end, rather than blanketing the delicate, sweet fruit.

Preheat the oven to 180°C/350°F/Gas 5.

Cut the bottom off each pear and place upright in a shallow ovenproof dish. Pour over the marsala and sprinkle over the brown sugar and cinnamon. Cut the vanilla pod in half lengthways and scrape the seeds into the dish along with the empty pod.

Bake for 30–40 minutes, or until the pears are soft. (You can check this by inserting a knife or skewer to see if it feels no resistance.)

Remove the pears from the oven and spoon over the syrup that has collected at the bottom. While the pears are still hot, grate over the chocolate so that it melts down the sides of the pear and slips into the sauce.

Serve the pears with the chocolate syrup poured over, and a dollop of crème fraîche if you like.

BLACKBERRY CLAFOUTIS

Serves 4

2 large eggs

100g caster sugar, plus
1 tbsp for the baking dish

1 vanilla pod

70g plain flour

200ml full-fat milk

250g blackberries

butter, for greasing

2 tbsp icing sugar, to serve

double cream, to serve
(optional)

This is one of the most straightforward and delicious puddings to throw together. It is essentially a pancake batter poured over fruit and baked in the oven until gloriously crisp and golden on top. The juice from the blackberries seep into the batter making little purple pockets. You can also use other seasonal fruit like plums, cherries or damsons.

Preheat the oven to 170°C/350°F/Gas 3½.

In a bowl, beat together the eggs and sugar. Halve the vanilla pod lengthways and scrape the seeds into the eggs. Sift over the flour and fold it into the mixture, then stir in the milk until you have a smooth batter. Set aside to rest for at least 10 minutes.

Butter an ovenproof dish and sprinkle with 1 tablespoon sugar. Strew the blackberries all over the bottom and pour the batter on top.

Bake in the oven for 40–50 minutes, or until the top is browned and slightly puffed up and a skewer inserted into the middle comes out clean.

Sift over the icing sugar, and serve with a bit of pouring cream too.

SUSSEX POND PUDDING

Serves 4–6

250g self-raising flour

125g chopped suet

200ml full-fat milk

200g unsalted butter, cubed

100g soft brown

100g caster sugar

1 lemon

double cream, to serve (optional)

This old-fashioned pudding is made by encasing a lemon in sweet, buttery suet pastry and steaming it for hours. It is incredibly warming for cold winter days. Once you've done the preparation, you can leave it to cook quietly while you get on with other things, so it is ideal for making ahead of time. All you need is a 1-litre pudding basin and a saucepan that comfortably holds it, preferably with a couple of centimetres to spare around the side.

Mix the flour and suet together in the pudding bowl. Make a well in the centre and pour in the milk. Using a spoon, stir the milk in the middle of the well so that the flour gradually incorporates into the liquid, eventually coming together to form a soft dough. If you need more liquid to collect the last bits of flour, add a little water, a tablespoon at a time. The main thing is to keep the dough fairly firm.

Gather the dough together and roll out to make a circle 1cm larger than the circumference of the pudding basin. Cut one-quarter out of the circle and set aside to use for the lid. Make the remaining dough into a cone shape and put it inside the bowl, pressing it against the sides to cover them, right up to the rim.

Put 50g of the butter into the bottom of the dough-lined bowl, then sprinkle over 25g of each of the sugars and set aside.

Using a skewer or larding needle, pierce deep holes all over the lemon to allow the juices to escape during cooking. Place the lemon on top of the layer of butter and sugar, then scatter the rest of the butter and sugar over and around the lemon. Cover with the remaining dough and pinch the sides together to seal well.

Take a large sheet of tin foil and fold a pleat down the centre. Place this over the top of the basin with the pleat running down the centre, allowing about 5cm down the sides, and seal tightly. (The pleat will enable the foil lid to expand as the pudding steams.) Wrap some kitchen

string around the side to hold the foil in place. Use extra string to make a handle for lifting the pudding in and out of the water.

Half-fill a saucepan with water and bring it to the boil. Gently lower the pudding basin into the saucepan. Turn the heat to medium and steam for 3 hours, topping up the water occasionally to ensure it doesn't evaporate completely — the water should come halfway up the basin.

After 3 hours, lift the pudding out of the pot and take off the foil. Slide a knife around the sides of the bowl and turn the pudding upside down on a plate. Serve piping hot with double cream drizzled on top.

CARDAMOM-SPICED RICE PUDDING *with* MANGO

Serves 4

100g short-grain or pudding rice

35g unsalted butter

50g caster sugar or vanilla sugar

4–6 cardamom pods, lightly crushed

1 vanilla pod, split

650ml (more if needed) full-fat milk

150ml double cream

a pinch of salt

1 mango

Inspired by flavours often found in sweet Indian desserts, this is a take on your typical rice pudding. Have some extra milk ready to add because the pudding may need more liquid than you think, depending on the heat of your oven and the size of your pot. Try using rice milk, soya or even goat's milk for non-dairy alternatives.

Preheat the oven to 150°C/300°F/Gas 2.

Rinse the rice well in cold water, drain and set aside.

In an ovenproof saucepan, over a medium heat, melt 25g of butter. Add the sugar and cardamom. Scrape the seeds from the vanilla pod into the saucepan with the rice. Pour over the milk and bring to the boil. Add the cream and salt and dot the surface with the remaining butter. Take off the heat, cover with foil or a lid and bake for 45 minutes.

Remove from the oven, stir gently then bake, covered, for a further 30 minutes. Stir again; you might need to add a little more milk at this point if it looks as though it is drying out. Scrape up any bits of rice that have stuck to the bottom.

At this point, if you prefer a pudding without a skin, cover the saucepan with a lid or foil; if you love the skin, leave it off. Bake for a further 1 hour, or until the rice is tender and creamy, though keep an eye on it to make sure it doesn't dry out – add some milk if it does.

Peel the mango and remove the stone. Chop into rough 1cm cubes. Serve the hot pudding with the mango sprinkled on top.

ROAST FIGS *with* MASCARPONE

Serves 4

8 ripe figs

125g mascarpone

1 tsp ground cinnamon

2 tbsp runny honey

zest and juice of 1 orange

20g walnuts,
roughly chopped

I love the simplicity of this delicious pudding. This is best made when fresh figs are available from late summer through autumn. The mascarpone melts into a creamy sauce surrounding the semi-collapsed, juicy roasted fruit.

Preheat the oven to 200°C/400°F/Gas 6.

Make a cross-shaped incision in each fig, slicing almost to the bottom but not cutting all the way through, and set aside.

Mix the mascarpone with the cinnamon, honey and orange zest.

Gently prise open the soft flesh of the figs. With a small teaspoon, scoop some mascarpone mixture into each fig, then lightly squeeze it shut again. Place the filled figs into an ovenproof dish. Sprinkle the figs with the walnuts and pour the orange juice over the top. Transfer to the oven and roast for 15–25 minutes, or until the figs are soft and collapsing.

TIRAMISU

Serves 6

4 egg yolks

150g caster sugar, reserving
1 tbsp for the coffee

250g mascarpone

100ml dark rum or
marsala

2 egg whites

175g Savoiardi sponge
fingers

300ml very strong coffee

1 tbsp cocoa powder

20g good-quality dark
chocolate, to grate
(optional)

This is one of my favourite Italian desserts — a kind of creamy trifle laced with chocolate and coffee. It tastes much better when it's made in advance, and the sponge fingers have had time to soak in all the flavours. You will need a serving dish measuring 26cm x 18cm x 4cm to ensure it holds two layers of fingers.

Beat the egg yolks and the sugar together in a bowl until they become pale and thick. Fold in the mascarpone and 50ml of the rum.

In another clean, grease-free bowl, beat the egg whites until they form soft peaks. Fold the egg whites carefully into the mascarpone cream.

Arrange half of the sponge fingers in the bottom of the dish to cover.

Mix the remaining 50ml rum and the reserved tablespoon of sugar into the coffee and pour half of it evenly over the sponge fingers, soaking them all thoroughly.

Spoon half of the mascarpone cream over the soaked sponge fingers and smooth to cover.

Lay the other half of the remaining fingers on top and pour over the rest of the coffee to soak them as before.

Finally, spoon over the remaining mascarpone cream to cover the surface completely. Cover and refrigerate for at least 3 hours.

To serve, sift cocoa powder all over the top. This dish also tastes wonderful with dark chocolate grated over the cocoa.

CHOCOLATE *and* ORANGE POTS

Makes 4

4 egg yolks

30g caster sugar

200ml double cream, plus
extra to serve (optional)

2 tbsp full-fat milk

zest of 1 orange

½ tsp ground cinnamon

1cm piece ginger, peeled
and grated

a pinch of sea salt

200g good-quality dark
chocolate, broken into
small pieces

*Gently spiced and rich yet surprisingly light, these little pots are the
ultimate chocolate dessert. Eat them hot, straight from the oven
or make them in advance and serve them at room temperature.*

Preheat the oven to 150°C/300°F/Gas 2.

In a bowl, by hand or using a mixer if you have one, whisk together the
egg yolks and sugar, until pale and fluffy. The consistency to aim for is
when a thread of the mixture, drizzled back into the bowl, holds onto
the surface for a second. (This is known as ribbon consistency.)

Put the cream, milk, orange zest, cinnamon, ginger and pinch of salt
into a saucepan over a medium heat and bring to a simmer. Remove
from the heat. Add the chocolate pieces, stirring them in so they melt
smoothly into the warm cream mixture.

Pour the melted chocolate cream into the beaten eggs and gently fold
it together.

Divide the chocolate mixture between individual ramekins and place
them in a baking tray. Add hot water to come halfway up the sides of the
ramekins then cover the whole tray tightly with foil, shiny-side down.
(This will help keep in the moisture and prevent the top forming a hard
crust.) Bake in the oven for 20–30 minutes, then carefully remove
the foil to check if they look set – they should be a little wobbly in the
middle. Different ovens really can make a difference to the time it takes
to cook, so don't be concerned if your pots need a little longer.

Remove from the oven and eat hot or, if you prefer them cold, allow
to cool and then refrigerate.

Serve with a little extra cream or crème fraîche, if you like.

BASICS

A few things that will always come in handy

BASIC RECIPES

YOGHURT SAUCES

These healthy, creamy sauces are great served with everything from lentils and pilafs to spicy meat dishes. The cucumber raita will cool a hot dish while the harissa yoghurt will add a spicy kick. I like using Greek yoghurt but regular yoghurt will also do.

Cucumber raita
½ cucumber, peeled, deseeded and grated
250ml yoghurt
1 garlic clove, crushed to a paste with salt
10g mint leaves, finely chopped
salt and freshly ground black pepper

Squeeze out any excess water from the grated cucumber. Put the cucumber in a bowl with the yoghurt, garlic, mint and mix well. Season to taste and serve.

Cumin and coriander yoghurt
250ml yoghurt
3 tsp ground cumin
10g coriander, finely chopped
salt and freshly ground black pepper

Mix the ingredients together in a bowl and season well.

I sometimes make a type of lassi drink with any that is left over. Just add ice cubes or chilled water and blitz.

Tahini yoghurt

2 tbsp tahini paste

1 garlic clove, crushed to a paste with salt

juice of ½ lemon

250ml yoghurt

salt and freshly ground black pepper

1 tbsp toasted sesame seeds (optional)

Mix the tahini with the garlic and lemon juice in a bowl. It will become quite thick. Add the yoghurt a spoonful at a time, mixing well to make a smooth paste. Season with salt and pepper.

Sprinkle over the sesame seeds to serve, if using.

Harissa yoghurt

250ml yoghurt

1 garlic clove, crushed to a paste with salt

2 tbsp harissa

salt

Mix all the ingredients together in a bowl, adding more or less harissa to suit your taste.

STOCK

Making a home-made stock takes up to 1½ hours, but most of that time is spent leaving it alone to simmer. Home-made stock is always much tastier than a stock cube and, what's more, it's much cheaper. Most of the ingredients you will have already — a few vegetables and herbs — and it's also a fantastic way to use up leftover bones from a roast.

Stock also freezes well, so make it in large quantities. Use what you need and then freeze the rest in sealed containers, taking it out to thaw as and when you need it.

Chicken stock

Chicken stock is a good all-round stock that I often use. If you can get them, throw chicken giblets into the stock, too. You can easily adapt this recipe if you want to make beef, lamb or veal stock. Just substitute 1.5kg of meat bones for the chicken.

Makes about 2 litres

2 chicken carcasses, raw or roasted

1 large onion, peeled and halved

2 carrots, peeled and chopped

4 celery stalks, chopped into large pieces

a small bunch of parsley stalks

2 bay leaves

a small bunch of thyme

6 black peppercorns

salt

Put all the ingredients (except the salt) into a very large pan and cover with at least 2 litres of cold water. Bring to the boil and skim off any scum as it rises to the surface. Lower the heat and simmer gently for about 1 hour.

Strain the stock into a large bowl. Discard the solid ingredients and season the stock with salt. Set aside to cool.

If you prefer a stronger-tasting stock, strain and return it to the pan but don't add any salt. Boil to reduce by half, then add salt after you've reduced it.

Once cooled, skim off any fat that has come to the surface and refrigerate to use within 2 days, or freeze for up to 2 months.

Vegetable stock

This light and aromatic vegetable stock makes an excellent foundation for any soup or stew.

Makes about 2 litres

1 large onion, peeled and halved

2 carrots, peeled and halved

4 celery stalks, chopped into large pieces

2 garlic cloves, peeled

1 fennel bulb, quartered

8 button mushrooms

1 tomato, halved

2 bay leaves

a small bunch of thyme

a small bunch of parsley stalks

8 black peppercorns

salt

Put all the ingredients except the salt into a large pan over a high heat and cover with just over 2 litres of cold water. Bring to the boil, then turn the heat down and simmer for 30 minutes. Strain, season with salt and leave to cool. Refrigerated, this will last for 3 days, or will freeze for up to 2 months.

Fish stock

When making fish stock I use the bones from white fish such as turbot, brill, monkfish or seabass as they produce a clear stock. The best place to obtain fish bones and heads is from your fishmonger.

Makes about 2 litres
2kg white fish bones and heads (excluding gills)
1 large onion, peeled and halved
1 carrot, peeled and cut into pieces
4 celery stalks, cut into large pieces
1 fennel bulb, quartered (optional)
2 bay leaves
a small bunch of parsley stalks
8 black peppercorns
salt

Put all the ingredients (except the salt) into a large pan over a high heat. Cover with just over 2 litres of water. Bring to the boil, skimming off any scum that rises to the surface. Lower the heat and simmer for 30 minutes. Strain, season with salt and leave to cool. Refrigerated, this will last for 2 days, or will freeze for up to 2 months.

SALAD IDEAS

A well-made salad is one of the freshest and most enjoyable things to eat. Buy whole lettuces and experiment with different textures and shapes. A salad made with good leaves doesn't need a complicated dressing – just a drizzle of lemon juice or vinegar and good-quality olive oil will do. Here are some ideas for salads, what you serve it with is completely up to you.

* Lemony sorrel makes a lovely addition to any salad, as do fresh herbs in general. I grow a little pot of herbs on the windowsill so I can snip some off as and when needed.

* For a substantial salad, just slice some raw vegetables: I like to use radishes, fennel, carrots or celery. Toss them together with parsley leaves and dress them with vinaigrette.

* Peppery watercress and rocket have an affinity and suit the stronger flavours of meat dishes.

* Chunks of iceberg lettuce with diced shallot, red wine vinegar and olive oil are delicious with fish or lighter plates.

VINAIGRETTES

Mustard vinaigrette

Here is a thick, mustardy dressing to drizzle over salads or to use as a sauce for dipping vegetables into. You can also try making it with other vinegars like balsamic or white wine vinegar.

1 garlic clove, crushed to a paste with salt
2 tsp Dijon mustard
1 tbsp red wine vinegar
90–120ml extra virgin olive oil
salt and freshly ground black pepper

If you've used a pestle and mortar to crush the garlic, you could make the vinaigrette in this. Otherwise, put the garlic in a bowl with the mustard. Whisk in the vinegar and then the oil, drop by drop at first, then in a steady, thin stream, as though making mayonnaise. When the mixture is emulsified, season well with salt and pepper.

A light, fresh vinaigrette

All you need here is lemon juice or a good wine vinegar.

1 tbsp lemon juice or red wine vinegar
90–120ml extra virgin olive oil
salt and freshly ground black pepper

Put all the ingredients into a bowl and whisk together well.

TECHNIQUES

Here are a few tips to help you get the best out of your ingredients.

Preparing meat

Knowing how to joint your meat, especially a bird, is a useful skill, and an easy one to learn. Place the bird breast-side up. Start by removing the leg, cutting through the skin where the thigh joins the body. Bend the leg back to dislocate the thigh bone from the socket and cut through the tendons to remove the leg joint entirely from the backbone and repeat with the other leg. Next detach the wings. Now separate the thigh from the drumstick by pulling back the joints in the same way and cutting neatly around the bone. To remove the breasts, slice down through the breast meat on either side of the breast bone and cut off the breasts leaving them attached to the rib bones. Lift the top of the carcass (with the breasts attached) upwards and cut through the rib bones to remove from the back part of the carcass.

All birds can be jointed the same way. It's worth knowing how to do this because it can be more economical to buy a whole bird than it is to buy all the pieces separately. That way, you can then use the carcass to make a stock as well.

You could also joint a whole cooked bird in this way when making the poached chicken with salsa verde (see page 64) or the roasted chicken over celeriac and potatoes (see page 176). Jointing it is easier than carving it into thin slices, and gives you juicier portions.

Browning meat

The key to a properly browned piece of meat is an extremely hot pan, whether you're quickly frying a steak or slow cooking a shoulder of lamb, you generally need to start by browning it. Searing the outer layer gives it that wonderful crust and colour, sealing in the juicy flavours and making it tastier and more appealing to look at.

Keep these hints in mind when browning meat:

* First heat the oil in your frying pan or casserole, then add the meat. If it's hot enough, it should sizzle when it touches the surface.

* Try not to overcrowd the pan because this will reduce the heat and cause the meat to stew rather than fry. If you have a large quantity of meat, brown it in small batches or use a larger pan.

Resting meat

When you're timing how long it takes to roast meat, don't just think of the cooking time. Allow at least half of that time again as resting time. This means a joint that takes 1 hour to cook will need half an hour to rest after cooking, before carving. Meat tenses up when heat is applied and the blood travels to the surface. Resting the cooked meat gives it time to relax again. The juices redistribute, making the joint more tender and succulent.

To keep meat from cooling down when it's resting, put it in a very low oven or cover it loosely with foil and leave in a warm place. Trust me, it is definitely worth the extra bit of time.

Sweating onions

Properly cooked onions are the foundation of many a great-tasting dish. But they do require a bit of time to transform from crunchy, pungent orbs to sweet, meltingly soft, golden strands.

This is a great example of the benefit of a good pan. A heavy pan with a thick base is the perfect vessel for cooking onions. The heat is evenly distributed so the onions don't burn easily. Once you feel confident with the amount of heat required – not too hot so they char, but not too low so they lie limp in the oil – you can leave them to cook, just giving them a stir every couple of minutes until they reach sweet, soft perfection. This process of 'sweating' the onions can take between 10 and 20 minutes, depending on your pan and the amount of heat.

Slow cooking vegetables for a soup base

Making a full-flavoured soup can often take a mere 30 minutes. But 20 minutes of this time should be spent making the base – the key to a delicious tasting soup. As with onions, the vegetable base needs some time on a low heat to get soft and sweet.

Chopped carrot, onion and celery are classic soup base ingredients because when they are slightly browned in a little oil they become sweet and intensely flavoured. But other vegetables can be cooked in the same way – both the courgette and white bean soup (see page 124) and the Mexican sweet corn soup (see page 96) are examples of the overall benefit gained from slowly cooking vegetables at the beginning. If you add salt at the start, you'll find your base tastes even better and you won't need to add much more salt later on.

Blanching, boiling

Whenever you're cooking pasta or blanching vegetables, remember to use plenty of water. Given lots of room to cook in, everything will cook faster and more efficiently. Using lots of water will prevent pasta from becoming soggy and starchy, and vegetables will keep more of their nutrients and colour. Remember to salt the water well to get the seasoning in early on.

Toasting spices

If you love spices and the aromas and flavours they produce, you will appreciate the results of toasting them and grinding them fresh. Certainly, you'll get the best out of them, but if you're short of time, you don't need to do this. Remember that you can buy spices whole rather than pre-ground, which stay fresh for longer.

To toast spices, place a small, dry pan over a medium-high heat and add your spices. Let them warm through until you start to hear them crackle and pop – it takes only a minute or so – then remove the spices immediately from the heat. Grind them in a pestle and mortar (or spice grinder).

Crushing garlic

Throughout the book, I refer to 'garlic crushed to a paste with salt'. Adding a pinch of salt helps to break the garlic down. This is something I usually find easier to do in a pestle and mortar. Otherwise, you can crush the garlic on a board. First, finely chop it, sprinkle with salt then, using the flat blade of a knife, crush the garlic and salt against the board until you have a smooth paste.

SUPPLIERS

Discovering great places to source ingredients makes cooking even more enjoyable. As does thoughtful shopping. Try to find your local specialists such as fishmongers, butchers and greengrocers, who will be able to give you guidance about what's in season or how to cook unfamiliar vegetables, fish or cuts of meat.

All of the ingredients found in this book are also available from most major supermarkets, but if you like to use independent suppliers or to buy some of your ingredients from specialist sources, the following websites will deliver throughout the UK.

Natoora

A specialist online supplier of food from independent producers. They stock fresh meat, including many of the less expensive cuts like cheek and oxtail (used in the pot-au-feu recipe), and vegetables, as well as some fresh fish. They also deliver excellent quality groceries such as artisan bread, cheeses and dairy, and store cupboard essentials like oils and spices.

www.natoora.com

FRESH FISH

If you don't have a local fishmonger or the supermarket doesn't offer what you need, Fish for Thought is an online supplier of sustainably sourced fresh fish.

www.fishforthought.co.uk

HERBS

Fresh herbs are so important to cook with, and if you use them often, it's worth growing your own. I always keep a pot or two on the windowsill of the herbs that are easy to grow — marjoram, basil, thyme and sage. Here are some sites that deliver specialist seeds or young plants to get going with:

www.rocketgardens.com
www.jekkasherbfarm.com

BREAD

Most bakeries don't offer online delivery so it's a good idea to find if there are any local to you to buy from direct. Otherwise, supermarkets are now starting to stock bread from good quality independent bakers, and many vegetable box suppliers can add artisan bread to your order.

Some of my favourite bread comes from the following bakeries:

London www.stjohngroup.uk.com   www.e5bakehouse.com

Leicestershire www.hambletonbakery.co.uk

Dorset www.longcrichelbakery.co.uk

Good ingredients are easy to find, and they'll make your food taste even better.

INDEX

A

anchovies 12
    baked peppers with mozzarella and
      anchovies 110
    salsa verde 64
    whole turbot roasted over potatoes
      and fennel 164
apples: pork chops with apple and
    fennel 48
artichokes
    globe artichokes 34, 130
    Jerusalem artichokes 66
asparagus
    braised spring vegetables with pearl
      barley 34
    risotto with asparagus, peas and
      lemon 26
aubergines
    baked aubergine with mozzarella,
      tomato and courgette 63
    Italian ragout of vegetables 146
    Middle Eastern aubergine and
      chickpeas 20
avgolemono – Greek chicken soup
    with lemon 98
avocados: quinoa salad with avocado,
    cucumber and chilli 137

B

banana and rum tarte tatin 192
barley
    barley, salted ricotta and tomato
      salad 136
    braised spring vegetables with pearl
      barley 34
    squash, chestnut and farro soup 28
basil
    courgette and white bean soup 124
    light summer soup with pistou 25
    pappa al pomodoro – tomato,
      bread and basil soup 126
beans 12
    borlotti beans 50, 56, 157
    broad beans 34, 118
    butter beans 140
    cannellini beans 124, 157
    green beans 25, 157
    runner beans 157, 170

beef
    beef meatballs in spiced tomato
      sauce 75
    pot-au-feu 178–179
    salt beef and dumplings 76
blackberry clafoutis 208
blanching/boiling vegetables 231
borlotti beans
    summer bean ragout with olives and
      herbs 157
    winter minestrone with pasta and
      beans 56
brassicas: spiced brassicas and
    chickpeas 31
bread/breadcrumbs 14
    baked aubergine with mozzarella,
      tomato and courgette 63
    endive and squash gratin 68
    pappa al pomodoro – tomato,
      bread and basil soup 126
broad beans
    braised spring vegetables with pearl
      barley 34
    broad bean and dill pilaf 118
browned butter 108
butter beans: Spanish butter bean and
    tuna salad 140

C

cabbage
    guinea fowl, cabbage and chestnut
      pie 180
    spiced brassicas and chickpeas 31
cannellini beans
    courgette and white bean soup 124
    summer bean ragout with olives and
      herbs 157
cardamom-spiced rice pudding with
    mango 213
carrots
    lamb harira with chickpeas 83
    lamb shanks with peas and
      gremolata 88
    medfoun – Moroccan New Year
      chicken with couscous 158
    poached chicken with salsa verde 64
    pot-au-feu 178–179
    roasted loin of venison with root
      vegetables 78
    in salads 228

salt beef and dumplings 76
    in stock 226–227
    warm salad of chard and
      chickpeas 145
    winter minestrone with pasta and
      beans 56
cauliflower
    cauliflower and potato curry 58
    spiced brassicas and chickpeas 31
celeriac: chicken roasted over celeriac
    and potatoes 174
chard
    fragrant and warming Thai noodle
      broth 22
    warm salad of chard and
      chickpeas 145
cheese
    blue cheese 106
    Cheddar 169
    feta 32, 136
    Gruyère 68
    mascarpone 214, 218
    mozzarella 63, 110
    Parmesan 26, 47, 63, 68, 100, 102
    ricotta 100, 136
chestnuts
    guinea fowl, cabbage and chestnut
      pie 180
    squash, chestnut and farro soup 28
chicken
    avgolemono – Greek chicken soup
      with lemon 98
    chicken biryani 173
    chicken roasted over celeriac and
      potatoes 174
    chicken tagine with preserved
      lemon, potato and olives 66
    chicken with new potatoes and
      lemon 44
    jointing 229–230
    medfoun – Moroccan New Year
      chicken with couscous 158
    poached chicken with salsa verde 64
chickpeas 12
    lamb harira with chickpeas 83
    Middle Eastern aubergine and
      chickpeas 20
    spiced brassicas and chickpeas 31
    warm salad of chard and chickpeas
      145
chillies 12, 13
    linguine with crab and chilli 112

mackerel with courgettes and
chilli 40
Mexican sweetcorn soup with
chipotle 96
quinoa salad with avocado,
cucumber and chilli 137

chocolate
baked pears with spices and
chocolate 206
chocolate and orange pots 220
tiramisu 218

clams
fish chowder 152
fish stew 61
seafood paella 162
steamed mussels and clams with
fresh tomato 37

cod: fish pie 169

cornichons: potato, cornichon and
mustard salad 134

courgettes
baked aubergine with mozzarella,
tomato and courgette 63
courgette and herb frittata 32
courgette and white bean soup 124
courgettes stuffed with spiced
lamb 84
light summer soup with pistou 25
mackerel with courgettes and
chilli 40

crab: linguine with crab and chilli 112

cucumber
cucumber raita 224
quinoa salad with avocado,
cucumber and chilli 137
soba noodle salad 142

D

date and orange cake 198

dhal 116

dressings: vinaigrette 130, 137, 228:
see also sauces

E

eggs
avgolemono – Greek chicken soup
with lemon 98
baked eggs with spinach and blue
cheese 106
courgette and herb frittata 32
Turkish-style baked eggs with
tomatoes 108

endive and squash gratin 68

equipment 8–10

F

farro
braised spring vegetables with pearl
barley 34

squash, chestnut and farro soup 28

fennel
fish stew 61
pork chops with apple and
fennel 48
in salads 228
in stock 226–227
whole turbot roasted over
potatoes and fennel 164

figs: roast figs with mascarpone 214

fish
brill 164
cod 169
haddock 152
hake 38, 61
halibut 38, 162
kingfish 170
mackerel 40
monkfish 162
pollock 169
salmon 169
sea bass 61
smoked haddock 152, 169
squid 154, 162
tuna 140
turbot 164
see also shellfish

fish chowder 152

fish pie 169

fish stew 61

G

garlic 13, 232

ginger: rhubarb fool with stem
ginger 196

globe artichokes
braised spring vegetables with
pearl barley 34
globe artichokes with
vinaigrette 130

grains 11
barley 28, 34, 136
farro 28, 34
quinoa 137

green beans
light summer soup with pistou 25
summer bean ragout with olives and
herbs 157

gremolata
lamb shanks with peas and
gremolata 88
mackerel with courgettes and
chilli 38

guinea fowl, cabbage and chestnut
pie 180

H

haddock: fish chowder 152

hake
fish stew 61

Moroccan spiced fish with peppers
and potatoes 38

halibut
Moroccan spiced fish with peppers
and potatoes 38
seafood paella 162

harissa yoghurt 225

herbs 13–14
courgette and herb frittata 32
summer bean ragout with olives and
herbs 157

J

Jerusalem artichokes: chicken tagine
with preserved lemon, potato and
olives 66

K

kale
spiced brassicas and chickpeas 31
winter minestrone with pasta and
beans 56

L

lamb
braised lamb shoulder with
turnips 90
courgettes stuffed with spiced
lamb 84
lamb harira with chickpeas 83
lamb shanks with peas and
gremolata 88

lemongrass
strawberry and lemongrass jelly 190
fragrant and warming Thai noodle
broth 22

lemons 13
avgolemono – Greek chicken soup
with lemon 98
chicken tagine with preserved
lemon, potato and olives 66
chicken with new potatoes and
lemon 44
light, fresh vinaigrette 228
risotto with asparagus, peas and
lemon 26
spaghetti al limone 102
strawberries with frozen whipped
lemon cream 203
Sussex pond pudding 210–211

lentils: dhal 116

linguine with crab and chilli 112

M

mackerel with courgettes and chilli 40

mangoes
cardamom-spiced rice pudding
with mango 213
Keralan fish curry 170

mascarpone
    roast figs with mascarpone 214
    tiramisu 218

meat
    beef 75, 76, 178–179
    browning 230
    lamb 83, 84, 88, 90
    pork 48, 50, 73
    resting 230
    venison 78

meatballs: beef meatballs in spiced
    tomato sauce 75

medfoun – Moroccan New Year
    chicken with couscous 158

mozzarella
    baked aubergine with mozzarella,
      tomato and courgette 63
    baked peppers with mozzarella and
      anchovies 110

mushrooms
    fragrant and warming Thai noodle
      broth 22
    in stock 226–227

mussels
    fish chowder 152
    fish stew 61
    seafood paella 162
    steamed mussels and clams with
      fresh tomato 37

mustard
    mustard vinaigrette 228
    potato, cornichon and mustard
      salad 134

N

noodles
    fragrant and warming Thai noodle
      broth 22
    soba noodle salad 142

O

olive oil 11

olives
    chicken tagine with preserved
      lemon, potato and olives 66
    Morrocan spiced fish with peppers
      and potatoes 38
    Spanish butter bean and tuna
      salad 140
    summer bean ragout with olives
      and herbs 157

onions 13, 231

oranges
    chocolate and orange pots 220
    date and orange cake 198
    poached summer fruit salad 188
    roast figs with mascarpone 214

P

pak choy: fragrant and warming Thai
    noodle broth 22

pancetta: radicchio, red wine and
    pancetta risotto 47

pappa al pomodoro – tomato, bread
    and basil soup 126

Parmesan
    baked aubergine with mozzarella,
      tomato and courgette 63
    endive and squash gratin 68
    penne with cherry tomatoes and
      ricotta 100
    radicchio, red wine and pancetta
      risotto 47
    risotto with asparagus, peas and
      lemon 26
    spaghetti al limone 102

pasta
    linguine with crab and chilli 112
    penne with cherry tomatoes and
      ricotta 100
    spaghetti al limone 102
    winter minestrone with pasta and
      beans 56

pears: baked pears with spices and
    chocolate 206

peas
    braised spring vegetables with pearl
      barley 34
    lamb shanks with peas and
      gremolata 88
    light summer soup with pistou 25
    risotto with asparagus, peas and
      lemon 26

peppers
    baked peppers with mozzarella and
      anchovies 110
    Italian ragout of vegetables 146
    Moroccan spiced fish with peppers
      and potatoes 38
    seafood paella 162

pistou 25

pollock: fish pie 169

pork
    pork chops with apple and
      fennel 48
    pork cooked in milk with potatoes
      and sage 73
    sausages and beans 50

potatoes
    cauliflower and potato curry 58
    chicken roasted over celeriac and
      potatoes 174
    chicken tagine with preserved
      lemon, potato and olives 66
    chicken with new potatoes and
      lemon 44
    fish chowder 152
    fish stew 61
    Italian ragout of vegetables 146
    Moroccan spiced fish with peppers

and potatoes 38
poached chicken with salsa verde 64
pork cooked in milk with potatoes
    and sage 73
potato, cornichon and mustard
    salad 134
roasted loin of venison with root
    vegetables 78
whole turbot roasted over potatoes
    and fennel 164

pot-au-feu 178–179

prawns
    fish pie 169
    seafood paella 162

Q

quinoa salad with avocado, cucumber
    and chilli 137

R

radicchio, red wine and pancetta
    risotto 47

rhubarb fool with stem ginger 196

rice 11
    avgolemono – Greek chicken soup
      with lemon 98
    broad bean and dill pilaf 118
    cardamom-spiced rice pudding
      with mango 213
    chicken biryani 173
    rice noodles 22
    seafood paella 162
    see also risotto

ricotta
    barley, salted ricotta and tomato
      salad 136
    penne with cherry tomatoes and
      ricotta 100

risotto
    black risotto with squid 154
    radicchio, red wine and pancetta
      risotto 47
    risotto with asparagus, peas and
      lemon 26

runner beans
    Keralan fish curry 170
    summer bean ragout with olives and
      herbs 157

S

sage: pork cooked in milk with
    potatoes and sage 73

salads (savoury) 227–228
    barley, salted ricotta and tomato
      salad 136
    potato, cornichon and mustard
      salad 134
    quinoa salad with avocado,
      cucumber and chilli 137
    soba noodle salad 142

Spanish butter bean and tuna salad
140
warm salad of chard and chickpeas
145
salads (sweet): poached summer fruit
salad 188
salmon: fish pie 169
salsa verde 64
salt beef and dumplings 76
sauces
cucumber raita 224
cumin and coriander yoghurt 224
pistou 25
salsa verde 64
spiced tomato sauce 75
see also vinaigrette
sausages and beans 50
scallops: seafood paella 162
sea bass: fish stew 61
seafood paella 162
shellfish
clams 37, 61, 152, 162
crab 112
mussels 37, 61, 152, 162
prawns 162, 169
scallops 162
soups
avgolemono – Greek chicken soup
with lemon 98
courgette and white bean soup 124
fragrant and warming Thai noodle
broth 22
lamb harira with chickpeas 83
light summer soup with pistou 25
Mexican sweetcorn soup with
chipotle 96
pappa al pomodoro – tomato,
bread and basil soup 126
squash, chestnut and farro soup 28
vegetable base for 231
winter minestrone with pasta and
beans 56
spaghetti al limone 102
spices 12, 232
spinach
baked eggs with spinach and blue
cheese 106
dhal 116
fish pie 169
salt beef and dumplings 76
squashes
endive and squash gratin 68
squash, chestnut and farro soup 28
squid
black risotto with squid 154
seafood paella 162
stock 14, 225–227
chicken 225–226
fish 227
meat 225–226
vegetable 226–227

store cupboard 11–12
strawberries with frozen whipped
lemon cream 203
strawberry and lemongrass jelly 190
Sussex pond pudding 210–211
sweetcorn
fish chowder 152
Mexican sweetcorn soup with
chipotle 96

T

tahini 12
tahini yoghurt 225
warm salad of chard and chickpeas
145
tiramisu 218
tomatoes 12
baked aubergine with mozzarella,
tomato and courgette 63
baked peppers with mozzarella and
anchovies 110
barley, salted ricotta and tomato
salad 136
beef meatballs in spiced tomato
sauce 75
cauliflower and potato curry 58
dhal 116
fish stew 61
Italian ragout of vegetables 146
lamb harira with chickpeas 83
Middle Eastern aubergine and
chickpeas 20
Moroccan spiced fish with peppers
and potatoes 38
pappa al pomodoro – tomato,
bread and basil soup 126
penne with cherry tomatoes and
ricotta 100
pot-au-feu 178–179
Spanish butter bean and tuna salad
140
steamed mussels and clams with
fresh tomato 37
in stock 226–227
summer bean ragout with olives and
herbs 157
Turkish-style baked eggs with
tomatoes 108
whole turbot roasted over potatoes
and fennel 164
winter minestrone with pasta and
beans 56
tuna: Spanish butter bean and tuna
salad 140
turbot: whole turbot roasted over
potatoes and fennel 164
turnips
braised lamb shoulder with turnips
90
pot-au-feu 178–179

V

vegetable dishes: *see under individual
vegetables*
venison: roasted loin of venison with
root vegetables 78
vinaigrette 10, 228
globe artichokes with
vinaigrette 130
light, fresh vinaigrette 228
mustard vinaigrette 228
quinoa salad with avocado,
cucumber and chilli 137

W

water chestnuts: fragrant and warming
Thai noodle broth 22
watermelon granita 202

Y

yoghurt 224–225
cucumber raita 224
cumin and coriander yoghurt 224
harissa yoghurt 225
mint yoghurt 84
tahini yoghurt 225

ACKNOWLEDGEMENTS

Among the many people I'd like to thank are my parents, family and friends for being such enthusiastic tasters and testers, and especially my mother for getting me into food and cooking in the first place.

The wonderful Amanda Harris at Orion for commissioning my book. Kate Wanwimolruk, my editor, for cheerful and tireless attention to detail. Julyan Bayes for his thoughtful design and everyone in the team at Orion.

Thank you Simon Wheeler, who took all the beautiful photographs of every single recipe we cooked and Claire Ptak for all the fun, encouragement, help and style she brought to the photo shoots.

A huge thanks to all the restaurants where I have worked for the passion, knowledge and inspiration they gave me and where my love of cooking grew. Especially Sam and Sam Clark at Moro, who taught me so much at the beginning of my life in the kitchen, Ruthie Rogers and Rose Gray at the River Café, a place which still feels like a home, and Fergus Henderson and the chefs at St John.

Finally for my two chief testers Leslie and Zoe and for those whom I enjoy cooking and eating with the most, especially Rupert, Joseph, Stevie, Tommi and Hugo.